TALES OF MOORLAND AND ESTUARY

Henry Williamson's stories of English wild life written after the Great War of 1914–18 are considered by many to be his finest work. The small villages of Devon, set between the Severn Estuary to the north and the rivers of Dartmoor to the south, provide the well known setting for this collection of tales about birds, animals, fish and the country people who lived there. Written throughout the period when Williamson was at work on TARKA THE OTTER, the tales are harsh, often highlighting the difficulties of rural life. Yet their truth of detail gives an astonishing indication of Williamson's remarkable attunement with the English countryside and wild life. He can truly be said to have achieved his 'ambition to bring the sight of water, tree, fish, sky and other life onto paper'.

Born in December 1895, Henry Williamson died in August 1977. The last great visionary of his generation, he was a man much loved, much misunderstood, and a writer by turns neglected and famous. Apart from his animal narratives he wrote direct accounts of his own life in rural Norfolk and Devon, numerous short stories, and two semi-autobiographical groups of novels – THE FLAX OF DREAM and the massive fifteen-volume CHRONICLE OF ANCIENT SUNLIGHT.

HERITAGE
TALES OF MOORLAND & ESTUARY

Henry Williamson

Macdonald Futura Publishers

A Futura Book

First published in Great Britain in 1953 by
Macdonald and Company (Publishers) Limited

First Futura edition 1981
Copyright © Henry Williamson

ISBN: 0 7088 2107 3

Photoset by
Rowland Phototypesetting Ltd
Bury St Edmunds, Suffolk.
Printed and bound in Great Britain by
©ollins, Glasgow

The cover shows 'A Dell in Devonshire' by Miles Birket Foster
    in the Victoria and Albert Museum (Cooper-Bridgeman)

Macdonald Futura Publishers Limited
Paulton House
8 Shepherdess Walk
London N1 7LW

PREFACE

These stories had to wait some considerable time—nearly three decades, indeed!—before they were published in book form by Macdonald & Co. The earliest was written in 1923—two years before my marriage. This was *The Yellow Boots*. I wrote it after reading in a local paper that an entire pack of hounds had, after being lost in fog during a chase on Dartmoor, been poisoned by the Master as soon as they returned to kennels. He had not waited even to inform the Hunt Committee which owned the pack.

The Crake had a filleted appearance in one number of the U.S.A. magazine, the bogus *Esquire*. In fact, not only was my story extensively cut, but entirely rewritten until it became a parody of what I had written. It was done without permission, too; and when I wrote and protested to the Chicago editor, an explanation was made that the 'reader', or re-write man, was a confirmed alcoholic who no longer worked for that florid periodical.

In 1926 I set myself to assemble the final version of *Tarka*, writing all night while nursing a sick baby and wife. It took about six weeks of exhausting labour. *Tarka* appeared in 1927: it brought fame in 1928, while I was composing the ultimate novel (*The Pathway*) of my youthful tetralogy called 'The Flax of Dream'.

That novel, published in October, 1928, brought many visitors on a pilgrimage to see the author. I was then herding various village sketches and stories into two books: *Tales of a Devon Village*, and *Life in a Devon Village*. Thus ended my first seven years in Ham, the original name of that village; and not so long afterwards a new-broom incumbent from a London suburb glorified it to Ham St.

George. This didn't last even so long as the small years of his rectorship.

Shaking the dust of rectorial criticism of *The Pathway* from my shoes, I took the family of two small sons to live beside a trout stream descending from Exmoor through the Bray valley and to pass by a thatched house called Shallowford. There I composed a rather silly volume, a sort of bogus guide and walking-tour affair, with characters more appropriate to 'Beachcomber's' column in the *Daily Express* than a serious book. It was an 'I-I-I' book; that is, narrated by my then satirical self. This concoction was called *Devon Holiday*. It contained some short stories, which now reappear between these covers.

Life at Shallowford was, at first, all bits and pieces. Frustration was my lot: I had been paid a fairly large sum of money by Dick de la Mare, of Messrs. Faber & Faber to write a companion book to *Tarka*. About a trout? A salmon? I hadn't the slightest idea what to write. I became irritable and moody. Months passed, and became years. I spent much of my time with a 2-ounce fly rod, wading up a 2-mile beat of the rocky river Bray. I bought several hundred Loch Leven trout from the fish-farm below Dulverton, and put them in the river; not to be caught, but to bring back grace to an over-fished stream. I watched for salmon, during freshets, from several places on the river banks, including a big alder tree. Downstream were several near-impassable weirs, each built to contain a flow of reservoir water: to be led-off by leats, or narrow ducts, to grist mills still being worked, for the grinding, between millstones, of barley—the chief food of bacon-pigs.

And so the summers went on; to be lost in the mists of autumn, the cold river flowing fast, outside our cottage standing below hill plantations of larch and spruce. All the rooms were sunless during six or seven weeks at the dead-end of the year, in our frosty valley.

One winter night the first paragraph of *Salar the Salmon* was written. It was now the New Year of 1935, six years after we had moved to Shallowford. Since 1929 a daughter and another boy had joined the two small brothers; and a fifth child was on the way. I continued the writing of the book day after day. It seemed dull to me; 'every word chipped from the breast-bone', as V. M. Yeates wrote of himself while writing, at Eltham in Kent, his classic *Winged Victory*. Almost uncaringly I saw the sun's rim appear over the tree-tops; the white rime of winter's dark melted on the two lawns, each set with its yew tree; fuller light came in the sky with the swallows home again; then, in early May, an annoyance of cuckoos was calling and gabbling from tree to tree in the Deer Park through which ran clear cold moorland water in which salmon leapt at dawn, and again at twilight. My rod remained in its stand: I left for my field above Ham village, to write in the hut, or outside in the blazing sun of June . . . July . . .

Chapters went off, uncorrected, to the publishers in London; thence to Plymouth to be set-up in page-proof by the printers. Page-proofs meant that no excisions could be made, or paragraphs added. I felt cold in the August sun sitting day after day beside a small pine tree, feeding myself occasionally on biscuits and cheese—and feeling that if Salar did not die soon, the author would: a deserved death, for surely it was the dullest prose ever written.

The book was published two months later, and sold well at once, with splendid reviews. I did not care; there had been too much anxiety; I must change my life—

So the family migrated to Norfolk, to start a new life; I to became a jolly red-faced chuckling extrovert farmer on 240 derelict acres. But in Norfolk, with little capital, the wages had to be paid from money earned at night by B.B.C. scripts on farming, and articles in the *Daily Express*, while by day one learned to use the body in tasks of remaking roads, rebuilding 'condemned' cottages; ploughing, making seed-beds, and selling barley at a loss—for it was, in 1937–39, the greatest slump in British farming for 150 years.

So we dug and loaded into an old lorry over 1700 tons of gravel and chalk; then, besides working in the fields, our team of four hauled hundreds of tons of mud from choked meadow-dykes dividing five grazing meadows, and spread a splendid compost on the arable. For years the meadows had been white with thistle-floss in summer and water-logged in winter; now they were drained, and bullocks grazed revitalized pasture between April and October, before going into the yards to be fattened.

Thus I worked the body hard during eight years; five of them during the Second World War which confirmed my ideas of the white races going wrong.

Almost ended was my little trade with British magazines. All of the war ended in general chaos.

But in the U.S.A. an outstanding magazine of quality managed to survive: and I must record my gratitude to *The Atlantic Monthly* which published half-a-dozen or so of the short stories during those war years; and for sending to the family parcels of food, which, during those dark days, were shared with town friends who were less fortunate than ourselves.

THE CRAKE

It is a wonderful feeling a man has when he is exploring a country for the first time, especially when he is young, with a war behind him, put away, he thinks, for ever. He is in a new country; he is a writer with the highest ambition; he lives in a thatched cottage said to have been built in the reign of King John, for a rent of eighteen pence a week.

Everything he sees and hears (when it is not about himself) is tremendously interesting, and forming into stories. The wild, beautiful, unexplored Atlantic seaboard! The falcons, the badgers, the otters, the character of the people! When he sits down to the table, the stories write themselves, out of his excitements.

That is the feeling I had when, one morning in the time of primroses and celandines in the hedge banks, and gloss on the coats of grass-feeding red Devon cattle, I left my cottage, spurning to lock the door, and with stick in hand set out to explore the fishing village across the estuary. The way led down the valley for a mile or so until there was a sharp bend in the lane where a little stream ran across the road—Forda, the little ford—and at the turn I went up another lane and past a farmhouse lying under the hill which I looked forward to climbing.

That farm and the outbuildings was a place to linger by. White owls nested under the thatched roof of the cart-shed; there was a pound-house where in autumn a horse turned a great cogged wheel which ground apples in a circular stone trough for the making of cider; and the men about the farm were so friendly. They seemed willing for a talk. I was not merely wasting their time, for in those days a motor-car in the lanes was a rare sight, and if the village had half a dozen visitors in the summer months it was said that "the place was opening-up-of quite a lot."

But no one was about this fine morning, and my destination was the estuary. The way led up a steep and narrow lane, or rather gulley, for its stony bed was a-trickle with water, as one entered a dark tunnel under blackthorn bushes. The lane, sunken below the fields on either side, was used only by dogs, drovers and cattle. It was too steep for a horse and butt, so there was little need to cut back the thorns and brambles which nearly choked the way. Higher up, hazel and ash clumps met overhead and made it a place of shade and sun in dapple and glister. I had been told that it was a disused sled-track: that years ago sacks of flailed corn were brought up and spread on the hilltop, for the winds to winnow off the doust, or shucks.

It was a steady pull up the lane, but at the top there was bright reward. I stood in the clear air of morning gazing over hundreds of square miles of land and sea. Far below, spread out like a model contour map, where the sandhills of the Burrows, blown by the sea-winds into a desert extending behind a shallow shore. A long headland enclosed the southern ocean, ending at Harty Point. There, across the steely-blue sea, on the horizon of sky and ocean, was Lundy, standing high; its cliffs, like those of the promontory, seen in clear detail in the low rays of the eastern sun. My watch said seven o'clock, but the world had been fresh and bright for over two hours. Across the Burrows I saw the white stalk of the lighthouse, among sandhills this side of the estuary of the Two Rivers: and across the water, the village which was my destination, built around the base of a green hill.

Usually I walked between twelve and fifteen miles every day. The thought of being indoors was unbearable. With happy anticipation I gazed at the route before me, of the miles along broad sands in which the ribs of wooden ships were embedded.

Descending the hill, I crossed the sandhills, and soon

was walking in the spindrift at the edge of the sea. For a change, I traversed the sands, with their shells of razor-fish and cockle, and walked along the upper-tide-lines among the corks and feathers and notched skeletons of birds struck down and plucked by the peregrine falcons. There were pink crab shells and sand-blasted bottles, dry seaweed thongs and barnacle-riddled driftwood, among which ran the ring-plovers upon stone and shell, piping their frail cries as they arose in flight before one; and after a swift wing-jerking circular flight they would glide to their feet again, to stand as still as the stones and watch the stranger whose bare feet were purring in the dry sand above the tide-line, where they were dreaming of laying their eggs.

Beyond the wrack-strewn hollows in the breaches of the sandhills lay the estuary, with waves breaking white on the submerged shoal called the South Tail. As I strode along the shore, still carrying my shoes, I saw oyster-catchers on a shingle bank; and rounding Aery Point, was soon trudging on wet loose gravel to the lighthouse, and thence upon the lower rocks, among pools where crabs hurried from my shadow, and strange small fish, locked in by the lapsed tide, reamed into the dark, seaweed-haunted depths. I was making for the middle ridge from where a waved handkerchief would bring a boat from the far shore, to row the traveller across the estuary for a shilling.

Such is a walk on a spring morning, when a man is free and facing life with zest: a timeless walk, every moment lived in peace; a walk that seems to go on for ever, and then it is all behind one, but living in the mind, timelessly.

2

I had made two previous visits to the village, the first by way of the mossy pans behind the sandhills, the second along the shore. Now, on my third visit, I felt that it was already a particular place of my own. The village was said to be natural and wild. That suited me! There were seventeen inns and taverns in its narrow wandering streets and along its quays. Each was filled, after the day's work, with a life rich enough to stimulate any writer. There was never any drunkenness in the inns, but plenty of good fun and talk. The low-ceilinged rooms, with their bars, benches, settles, and tables were lit by oil-lamps. They were the social meeting-places of men who worked in the ship-yards, the boat-houses, and the fishermen whose lives were almost entirely lived in thoughts of salmon.

There were sailors, too, some of them from the Baltic, the Indian Ocean, the China Sea. Steam had brought most of them; but an occasional three-masted timber-ship from Finland or Scandinavia sailed over the bar on the spring-tides, the extra depth of water floating them up the river to Bideford.

The scene that met my eyes on that early spring day was one that by now was becoming part of my new and wonderful life. The steep, wave-wet slip, grown with seaweed below, led up from a rocky foreshore littered with old pots and pans, fish-heads, rusty bicycle frames, and other jettisoned rubbish; dark salmon nets hanging on walls during repairs; fishermen working at them, clad in dark-blue jerseys, salt-encrusted trousers, bare-footed like the children. The Seamen's Mission, with its biblical text painted over the door, and a lonely looking Lascar, face more green than brown, disconsolately standing against the wall outside. The chemist's shop with the big blue and red globes of coloured water in the window and the little corked phials of odd objects blanched in alcohol—a viper, a frog with two heads, a sea-horse, a lamprey. The ship-chandler's with the copper and brass fittings displayed in the window, with splendid new port and starboard lamps in polished phosphor-bronze which did not corrode in salt water; the anchors, boathooks, and yacht's fenders, the neat coils of Manila rope.

Having had my fill of staring, I padded back the way I had come, up and down narrow sett-stone streets filled with the shouts and happy cries of scores of bare-footed children. I was making for the Royal George. On the way thither I had to pass the War Memorial, the design of which, I felt with relief, was no oppression of the spirit. There were upon it no winged seraphs holding aloft torches or swords; no draped female figures with ecstatic or selfrighteous faces gazed into the sky. Such memorials were common elsewhere in Britain at that time: the commissioned, directed work of third-rate pretentious sculptors obeying the wishes of committees dictating the disposal of the subscribed money. They reflected not the truth of men who had died, but only commonplace civilian feeling unaware of its own sentimental obscurity.

While my twenty-four-year-old self was musing thus, standing by the plain cross and thinking of my friends of long ago, I noticed and old man walking slowly towards the memorial from another direction. He looked to be much worn by the sea. The elements had long since taken the dye out of shapeless peaked cap and jersey alike; the eyes which looked at me out of the round face were vacant, a faded blue, the lower lids fallen and red. To the tops of his legs he wore sea-boots of cracked leather, seemingly nearly as old as himself. They had been botched many times.

Seeing his eyes fixed on me, I bade him good morning, and with respect for his obvious great age and maritime experience I saluted him with my right hand.

He made no reply, but slowly raised a finger to the peak of his cap. Otherwise he continued to stand still. As he also continued to gaze at me, I bent down, as though intent upon reading the names on the memorial.

Nearly all the names were of sailors, lost in the Royal Navy and the Merchant Service. When I looked up again, the old man was still regarding me with his anxious eyes. At last he spoke.

"A man must splice a rope," he said.

"Yes, of course," I replied, while wondering what he meant.

About a quarter of an hour later, as I strolled barefoot upon the narrow sett-stoned way, I came upon a small cul-de-sac called Irsha Court. There I saw the old fellow again. He was pouring water out of a battered copper kettle into a tub. I noticed how it left the spout in a shaky splashing. Some of it had gone over his boots. Was that perhaps why he wore them?

The water in the tub was brown with dissolved essence of oak bark, in which the nets and sails of fishermen were preserved. The tub stood just outside the open door; but what took my fancy at once was a carved wooden woman, painted in blue and pink and black, fixed on the wall above the door. Figurehead of a sailing ship! It was startlingly beautiful, with all the mystery of remote deep water, of coral isle and the peaks of the Andes. Inside the cottage, in the single downstairs room, someone was at work on a net.

Now a stranger to what, for him, is an entirely new world often shows a curiosity which reveals his own gaping inexperience; and a young writer, of course, is always questing for material for his work. I took a quick glance into the room, which I felt to be a treasure-house of bygone age. Would there be stuffed and varnished flying fish, small brilliant birds of the tropics under glass domes? Strange sea-shells, perhaps the skin of a monkey, or a necklace of human teeth? A painted shield taken from the cannibal chief of a war-canoe among the islands of Polynesia? And, of course, models of full-rigged ships in bottles on the kitchen shelf.

Glancing in, I got a shock, Upon a chair sat a man with no ears. Part of his nose was missing. His jaw and cheeks and neck and hairless skull looked as though he had been made of wax and melted in fire.

"Oh, do forgive me," I said. "I have lost my way to the Royal George."

The apparition came to the door and pointed down the street, with an accompaniment of mumbled words and a kind of nasal whistling. I pretended gratitude for the information and hastened away.

3

As I drank my beer, and ate my lunch of bread and cheese and pickled onions in the Royal George, I learned from the landlord that the injured man was the only surviving son of the old fellow, who himself was one of the last of the deep-water sailors of the village. He was what the landlord called a masts-and-yards man. Four of his five sons had been lost at sea, three of them in the war. The fifth, and youngest, who lived with his father in Irsha Court, was known locally as Whistling Paddy. He had served in an oil-tanker, which had been torpedoed. When the crew had abandoned ship and taken to the boats a roar of flame and billowing smoke had suddenly arisen like forest fire in the dark Atlantic night. The boat crews had rowed desperately to escape the widening fringes of fire sliding down the slopes of the swell, and they were gaining on the roaring furnace when the tanker exploded, and flaming spirit had dropped out of the sky upon one of the boats in which Paddy had been rowing.

I gathered that, with his wound-gratuity paid recently, Whistling Paddy and his father had bought an old salmon boat from a certain fish agent, together with a net and, most important of all, a licence. They had had to pay a lot of money, for licences were coveted things, and limited in number by the Two Rivers' Conservancy Board.

Apparently the fish agent, who in some of his spare time was a preacher, had driven a hard bargain. But it is only fair to say that everything was scarce, and therefore dear, in those days immediately after the ending of the war.

Salmon were dear, too; and if the season, which no man
could foretell, turned out to be a good one, there would be
a fair return for the money, as the agent had declared,
quoting "Render unto Caesar the things which are
Caesar's", before his final "Take it or leave it, midear,
there be plenty others after my boat and gear, tidden no
odds to me who buys what an honest man has to sell."
After that business-like remark the fish agent had been
known as Julius Caesar.

With two others, out-of-work ex-service men (there
were many such at that time), a crew of four had been
assembled. One share for the boat, another for the net; and
a share for each of the four men. That was usual, and
considered fair. It meant that old Masts-and-Yards and
Paddy took two-thirds of the money paid for salmon by
the agent who bought the fish from the boats, paying the
best market price, wholesale, less a small commission for
the work of collecting the fish. Live and let live—the
principle that satisfied all in the village.

There was much speculation in the Royal George about
the wisdom of this particular venture. The licence cost five
pounds a season; the old man was beyond such heavy
work, while the son was a cripple, suffering at times,
particularly at the full of the moon, from headaches, which
made him feeble. He would be unable to haul properly on
a rope. It was during the spring tides, the biggest tides
coming with the new moon and again with the full moon,
that fish ran up better than on the neaps; and the spring
tides, it was thought, would prove too much for such a
crew of cripples and men ignorant of the currents.

The draughts from the lower estuary, shot from off the
sandbanks of the bar, were dangerous to those who did not
know how uncertain the swell could be there. Many a boat
had been swamped on the North and South Tails, upon
which a swell might roll in unawares, in calmest weather.
Apart from the danger, the work was hard, much harder
than they had bargained for. The old man was fit only to

chew tobacco with the stumps of his teeth and stand about on the quay in fine weather; he was too masterful, "he never took no advice, whether from doctor, parson, or them as knew the tides". What did he know about fishing? He had been a deep-water man all his born days, an old masts-and-yards man, who didn't understand shoaling water. But "'twadden no good tellin'm. He wouldn't listen to no man"!

I gathered that there was considerable animosity in the village between the fishermen and the water-bailiffs employed by the Conservancy Board. The Board was the legal authority which ruled when salmon-fishing should begin and when the season should end. It controlled the netting in salt water, and the rod-fishing in the fresh water of the rivers which flowed into the estuary. It decided the number of the boat licences, and the cost of licences for both nets and rods. Apparently netsmen had a deep grudge against the Board.

Angrily they told me of the differences between the season of netting in the sea, and that of fishing in the rivers. The rod-and-line men on the river-banks were allowed to fish for salmon and sea-trout a month before the nets were permitted to start; and at the back-end, or autumn, the nets were off a month before the rod-and-line men were stopped by law from fishing. In the eyes of the nestmen, to whom salmon were their living, this was unfair. You could take fish for sport eight weeks more in a season than for your living! Many a water-bailiff was, in imagination, thrown into the sea for that fancied injustice. Indeed, on one occasion, during netting, or poaching, in the close season, the bailiffs' boat was rammed in the Pool, in an attempt to upset and drown them, apparently.

There was more than the eight weeks, too. For whereas a poor man, they declared, had his living to get by hard work, he was restricted during the season to five days a week only; a rich man, a rod-and-line man, could fish six days a week, and six nights, too, if he'd a mind to! Ah,

there was one law for the rich, another for the poor!
Money talked! The water-baillies were there only to serve
the interests of the rich man, not those of the poor
fisherman.

What was the reason for the five days a week fishing for
the nets, I enquired; and my innocent question was
answered by a roar, and such angry looks, that I did not
repeat it in the Royal George. I had the answer, however, a
little later in the season.

4

There was a young doctor in the district who was also a
fly-fisherman. He did a lot of work, for a hobby, in
compiling a natural history of the Two Rivers. He
analysed the waters of the various streams which fed the
parent rivers coming from the southern watershed of Exmoor and the north-western slopes of Dartmoor. He collected in little close-mesh nets, the summer fish-food in
the rivers, comprising plankton, daphnia, nymphs, creepers, shrimps, snails, and other small forms of life. The
doctor believed that truth would always prevail with men,
were the facts presented to them in a way they could
comprehend. The rivers were the nurseries of the young
stock, and salmon were not unlimited in number.

Trying to do good, to replace ignorance and selfishness
with knowledge and co-operation, the doctor volunteered
to give a lecture in the village one night. He would like to
talk to the fishermen, to tell them about his adventures up
the rivers, which were the nurseries of the baby salmon.
Unless a proper number of mature fish were allowed to get
up the rivers to spawn, he said, the stock would decline
and die out—and the netsmen's livelihood with them.

The talk was sponsored by the Clerk to the Board. Bills
announcing the lecture on the Life Cycle of the

Salmonidae were posted about the village. Admission free. I made it my business to attend.

Knowing the habits of fishermen, the lecturer timed his talk to take place one evening when the tide was high, when all the netsmen would be ashore. Net fishing could be done only on the last of the ebb and the beginning of the flow, when the channels were narrow and the currents not too strong for the hauling of the nets.

The doctor was liked in the village. He played skittles in some of the inns with the men; he had brought many of their children into the world; he did not press for his bills to be paid. Because he was popular, many fishermen went to the Mission Hall to hear him, while determined not to accept a lot of book-stuff and words which had nothing to do with their necessity to earn money to buy food and clothes for the missus and kids. He might be a good doctor, and no man would say otherwise and not be contradicted, but did he know about salmon and peal? Had he ever worked in a crew, had he ever hauled a net, beyond giving a hand now and again when he was out messing about down the estuary? What could a mere water-whipper know about real fish-catching? Did he deny that salmon spawned in the gravel pits left on the Shrarshook by the gravel boats? Salmon, as all men knew, were salt-water fish, and so it was nature that they spawned in salt water! 'Twas a dirty lie, about laying their eggs in river water, a lie just to cheat the poor man of his living, so that rich gentry could have their sport whipping water, wi' hartifissal flies, up the valleys! Ah, they were not going to be sucked in by any old flimflam talk!

The doctor knew all this; but he remained cheerful, even confident. He had borrowed a magic lantern, and had some slides to throw on the screen made of a borrowed bed-sheet tacked up on the wall of the Mission House.

Before the assembled rugged faces, from which arose much rank tobacco smoke, the doctor began his lecture. He started by saying that he would tell them only of what

he had seen himself, and they ought to know him well
enough to know that he would not tell them any false-
hood. He had seen fish laying their eggs in the gravel beds,
called redds, of little brooks and runners far up under the
moors. These salmon, in spawning dress, were all colours.
The keepers, or cock fish, were usually red and yellow;
while the sows or hen-fish were usually dark brown, a
bronze colour.

He described the fighting among the male salmon; the
eels which attacked them when, weak after spawning, and
often covered with the same sort of yellow fungus which
attacked riverside trees, they were too feeble to make the
return journey to the sea. But if a salmon after spawning,
he said, could get down to salt water, perhaps as thin as a
sprat, yet with its silver coat come upon it again, it might
be restored to healthy life and growth.

"It cleans itself!" shouted a voice. "Us calls'n kelts,
midear!"

"Exactly!" agreed the doctor. After a while he went on.
"Now the eggs which hatch, usually in the early months
of the new year, turn into what we call alevins. They are
little fish with their egg-sacs, just like the yolk of a hen's
egg, shrinking into their bellies. Soon the alevin becomes a
fry, a tiny little spotted fish, looking just like a trout. It has
red and black spots, when only an inch long. It takes two
years of living in freshwater to grow to about six inches in
length, feeding on flies which have hatched, snails and
shrimps, in fact anything it can get. In this stage it is called a
parr. Alevin first, then fry, then parr. It feeds hungrily, in
competition with the native non-migratory brown trout
of the stream—and with the parr of the migratory sea-
trout, what you call peal, as well.

"Then, usually in the month of May, the parr in its third
year of river-growth begins to change into a smolt. Its
scales become silvery, and in some excitement it drops
down the river, to find the estuary and the sea. You must
have seen many smolts jumping in the Pool here, in May."

"Us have midear, us have! Go on, doctor, go on, us be waiting for 'ee!"

"Right! Grand little fellows, the smolt. Away to sea they go—if they survive their enemies in the estuary, that is. There are many bass waiting for them in the String, where the two rivers meet—you all know the String much better than I do, where the two ebb-tides meet and jabber against one another—well, if the smolt escape the bass and the cormorants they reach deeper water and grow rapidly as they eat the rich and strange food of the ocean. Some return after a few months, weighing four or five pounds. They are called grilse. Others stay longer in the Atlantic, and grow to great weights, eating prawns, herrings, and all sorts of smaller fish; but always, if they survive those greedy herring hogs and seals, they try to return to the rivers again, to spawn, and so to continue the race or species. If too many are lost in the sea, or when lying in the rivers—"

"Ah, they rod-and-line boogers!" roared a voice.

"Quite right!" said the doctor. "Some must be left to spawn, for stock fish! I agree with what you said, Billy. Now, with your permission, I propose to show you some magic-lantern slides of salmon scales. Here is the first one You will see that it is like the cross-section of a tree. Or like a thumb-print; but the likeness to a tree is better. These scales grow with the fish; they reveal its growth. This is one off a four-year-old fish. Observe those inner rings, evenly spread; they tell the growing period of the parr, of its first summer in the river, when food was plentiful. Beyond them, you see the rings are jammed up, clotted together, dark and thinly spaced: that is the winter period, when the fish made little or no growth, from little or no food. Now observe what happens to a scale when the fish reached the good food in the sea! Look at the expansion! If it wore one of those excellent jerseys knitted by your good wives, it would nearly burst it open! That was when the smolt began to gulp down shrimps, sprats, and anything it could get. That little bit of growth in the middle, the small rings in the inner scale, show the two years' river-feeding: these wide and wavy rings on the edge show the next two years' growth, for it remained two years in the sea—and grew to twenty-nine pounds' weight in that time! The first two years of the fish's life produced about three ounces of growth, in bone and flesh; the next two years, nearly thirty pounds! Wonderful, isn't it? Now then, I'll be pleased to answer any questions. Only remember—when I want to have a bathe I'll dive in by myself—I don't want any help this evening!"

There was a roar of laughter. The lights were turned up. The doctor began to pack a pipe, while sitting easily on the side of the lecturer's table, swing a leg.

"Come on, don't be shy! Ask anything you like."

No response.

"Why, what's happened? Have you all been hearing the Crake?"

It was perhaps not a tactful question; but the doctor was well pleased with himself, a little over-confident at the good humour of his audience. He felt he knew them, and that they would take what he said, from knowing him to be a 'proper chap'. They needed education; they were prejudiced, from ignorance; some even believed in that relic of superstition, the Crake, as a portent of death approaching one of themselves. Obviously it was some bird calling at night; but should the call or cry happen to coincide with a death by drowning, perhaps half the world away, when the news arrived, weeks afterwards perhaps, someone remembered that the Crake was heard about that time. Nonsense! Relic of the age of witch-hunting and mental darkness!

"Come on, chaps, let's hear from you. I don't know everything, but I'll do my best to answer any question."

Yes, they were a rough lot, but good boys when treated properly. Had they not been dead against the Tory candidate, all Liberal to a man until the Tory member of Parliament got them the right to have their votes, when they were at sea during an election, by proxy? In generosity for that, to a man they had turned Tory; and next time the Liberal candidate had come to address them, it was his turn to have flat tyres to his motorcar! And hadn't two police-men, not so long ago, been caught, in nets flung upon them as they walked side by side for safety at night, and soused in the sea, suspended in the net from the top of the quay? They thought the police were in league with the water-bailiffs to stop the poor man's right to take salmon in the closed season.

"Surely you must want to ask me something?"

At this point a burly individual got on his feet and spat carefully between his boots. This was Bob Kift, one of the strongest of the fishermen, who was usually most violent in his words about the water-baillies. Was he not the man who had actually, single-handed, dipped the two police-men in the net? He was a big-headed man, as powerful as a bull seal. Where his stretched and faded woollen jersey ended at his hairy wrists and massive neck his skin was almost as brown as a sail or net. He could eat a dozen herrings for his tea and then could manage a pound of steak, if he could get it. Eighteen stone of bone and meat, otherwise muscle, stood on feet encased in black rubber thigh-boots which were patched in places with red rubber motor-tyre patches. The human seal cleared his throat, but no words came.

"Well, Bob Kift, I didn't think you were a shy man!"

"Ooh, I ban't shy, doctor," replied Robert Kift. "I ban't shy, noomye! But 'ee zaid us could ask ee questions, didn't ee, surenuff?" He spoke softly.

"Certainly, Bob. Ask anything you like," replied the doctor, deceived by the softness of the big man's voice.

"Wull then," Bob Kift suddenly roared out, "what about they bliddy water-whippin' rod-and-line men kill-ing parr and stock fish with their bissley li'l bits o' fluffy feather and 'ooks up the rivers for a pastime?"

Shouts and bellows of laughter greeted the comedian.
Thus encouraged, the bull seal plunged to the attack. His
mouth wide open, so that his bristly grey moustache hid
most of his nose, he hollered, "Why should they dolled-up
niminypiminy loobeys be allowed to take the bread out o'
the' mouths o' our chillen? They gentry fishes for pleasure
only, while us does so for a living! Aye, 'tes true! They can
fish in March, when the big run o' fish be comin' in, but us
chaps has to wait till April! Tidden right! They stops the
nets in March, when the fish be runnin' plentiful, so that
salmon can get up the rivers, for to provide sport for the
rich man! If salmon spawn in autumn, there's plenty o'
sojers rinnin' up then, red as mullets, to keep the stock
goin'!"

"Red hake, you mean, don't you, Bob Kift?"

"Aye, red 'ake us has to call'm, like yippocrits, in the
close season, else us'd be fined or sent to gaol, if they
water-baillies had their way! And I'll tell 'ee this, midear,
for to put through your magic lantern when you'm showing it off to the gentry what sits on the Bench! Ask they
magistrates, what fines poor men for poachin', as they
calls it, ask they niminypiminy water-whippers if their
cooks 'ave ever bought red 'ake at the backdoor, for the
gentry to sit at their tables and eat at night! Why, if they
had their desserts, they'd all be in gaol, that's my question
to your answer, Doctor!" And the bull seal sat down.

The Mission Hall was in an uproar of laughter and
shouts, of stamped feet and rolling heads.

The doctor was a man of courage, which may be the
same thing as obstinacy at times. When the laughter had
subsided a little, and they were waiting for more fun, he
said, "Ah, Bob Kift, you ought to be on the Board, with
your eloquence! But now let's be serious a moment. If all
the fish are caught before they can spawn, your living, as
well as the river fishing, will simply die out. You are
agreed about that, surely? Come now!"

"Tidden true, you know," intoned a solemn voice.

They looked round, at the figure of Julius Caesar, the fish agent, who had risen on his feet. The audience at once settled quieter. They preferred Bob Kift to speak for them; but let a man have his say. And from what they knew of Julius Caesar, his say would be something.

"I have somep'n to say," said the solemn voice. Aye, it was coming, trust Julius Caesar. "The Lord put the fish into the sea, no man can deny that, durin' the creation of the earth in six days. Fish were created for the food o' men. Can anyone deny that?"

"What about seals and 'errin' 'ogs?" cried a voice from the back of the room.

"I ham concerned with the truth o' the Book, and let no man deny it except at the peril of his immortal soul, and the chanst o' hivverlastin' damnation." Julius Caesar looked around. All eyes avoided his eyes. "Wull then, since no man can deny the truth, I can illustrate what we have heard tonight by bringin' to you the miracle o' the loaves and fishes, which the Book—"

But the man who had mentioned seals and herring hogs, otherwise porpoises, did not appear to have any respect for Julius Caesar. He interrupted the threatened sermon by calling out, "Let they as be saved, or think they are, save their voices for Sundays! Meanwhile, why don't the Board shift they rocks below Middle Ridge? If they profess to be servin' the interests of the working man, why don't they clear away the rocks? Shall I tell you why? Because they care nothing for the workers, though they pretend to, like all capitalist yippocrits. It be a bourjois swindle, to keep down the Workers' Revolution. Lenin said—"

"Us don't want no red flag yurr, midear," cried Bob Kift, getting on his feet, "All the same, Doctor, there be some sense in gettin' the Board, if they'm a mind to it, to dredge up they rocks which tears the seines of your nets time and time agen. Now, Doctor, us knows 'ee, but with all respect, you ban't very old, midear, and some on us chaps have bin yurr saison after saison three score years and more. You'll do more good if you ask the Board to shift they rocks, but they won't tackle it, and shall I tell 'ee for why? Because they want netsmen to have broken nets, for to let the fish through, for their pals on the riverside upalong to get the fish!"

The noise of agreement was terrific. The meeting seemed to be out of control. Vainly the doctor's voice cried out that the Board had no money to undertake the work; that if the men wanted to do it, why didn't they do it themselves? The Board wasn't all-powerful; it merely tried to preserve the stock of fish for year after year . . . They went out noisily to the pubs. Nothing apparently had been achieved by the good intentions of the doctor.

When we were alone in the room, he said to me, "You won't get any objective thinking from men who still believe in such palpable superstition as the Crake."

I agreed with the doctor. Obviously they were as prejudiced as the limpets on the rocks.

In the Royal George I heard old Masts-and-Yards declaring that salmon did not spawn in the rivers; in his father's time, and grandfather's before him, he said, fish spawned on the gravel of the Middle Ridge, which some called Shrarshook, since Cap'n Charles Hook had bin drowned there in his young days by the Crake, but Middle Ridge was allus the proper name.

The old man's son, Whistling Paddy, sat beside him. I avoided speaking to him. I felt that he was shy of speaking, for he could not articulate his words properly, his jaws having been set askew after being broken by the torpedo explosion which had preceded the burning in petrol flames. Also, the ear of anyone he was confiding in was liable to be sprayed by a whistle of beer.

The trend of the talk was that someone had got at the doctor, someone on the Board, and sucked him in, ah, that was the only explanation, for he was a nice little fellow, who paid his way, and harmed no man by either word nor deed. The lecture was the subject of much talk that night;

but by the following week, when the season was opened, something was reported which put nearly everything else from their minds.

The Crake had been heard by three boat crews fishing from the Shrarshook, in the darkness. It was no exaggeration, it was a fact; a dozen men told me that they had heard it quite clearly in the darkness. The doctor laughed at the story. I did not know what to think.

Meanwhile, I was learning more about the art of salmon fishing.

5

The tides ruled when the netsmen could fish. Once every day and once every night the lunar Atlantic pulse moved up the estuary, filling the arms of the Two Rivers. The sea went up far beyond the old bridges of Barnstaple and Bideford, pressing back the fresh waters of the moorland rivers; and at the tide-heads, at the very end of ocean's impulse, the flow hesitated and became the ebb. Unless there was enough water in the rivers for the fish to run up farther, they returned with the tide, to come back again in the following flow. Each journey up and down the estuarine reaches was perilous for salmon; for when the tide was making, and again when it was nearly ebbed away, the boats went from their moorings below the sea-wall, each with its crew of four, to take salmon and peal in nets two hundred yards in length, each with a mesh of two inches, the size determined by law to permit the escape of immature fish.

6

It so happened that on the day of my next visit it was the turn of the boat owned by Whistling Paddy and skippered by his father (out of courtesy to the old man) to start the morning's fishing upon the sandbank of the dangerous shoal called the South Tail. The licensed boats of the estuary took turns at the various fishing places, so that all should have an equal chance. So the boat skippered by old Masts-and-Yards, its number painted on its bows according to the law, left its mooring below the Royal George in advance of the other boats and went down upon the massive green and wimpling glide of the ebb.

It was a spring tide; the moon was new; the weight of incoming press of water had made the currents the fastest of the month; the ebb was equally rapid. It swilled along down to the North and South Tails, marked by their successive lines of the dreaded white water.

With placid dips of sweeps the boat drifted down on the tide, passing a leaning buoy on which was perched a herring-gull with one leg. The bird was waiting for the water to lapse, for the wide expanse of the middle ridge to show itself. Then it would fly by custom thither, prise off mussels with its beak, carry them into the air, drop them on the stones below, and follow them down to eat out of the smashed shells. The pitiless yellow eye of the bird stared at the old sailor sitting on the piled net in the stern, who saw it without a thought.

Sometimes a wave, driven by the west wind, slapped against the bows of the boat, and skits of water were flung into it. Soon the buoy, marking the edge of the fairway, was left behind.

A mile and more seawards, waves were breaking on the tails of the bar with a dull and ceaseless roar. Beyond in the bay a tramp steamer was lying at anchor, awaiting the iron ball on the post by the lighthouse in the sandhills to arise, a sign that the bar was navigable. The ship would have to wait several hours for high water.

To left of the salmon boat was a ridge of grey pebbles, above which were low cliffs of sand worn by wind, the ragged dunes held by marram grasses. This was the Westwood Ho! Pebble Ridge, made famous by Kipling in *Stalky & Co*. The old man looked without interest at the long bleak stretch of sand; his mind was far away, perhaps looking upon scenes of the South Pacific, the green slopes of Peru, the immense towering Andes flushing pink in the sunrise which had not yet looked upon the top-s'ls of the three-masted schooner, whose holystoned decks he trod with his wooden shoon. He had worn these as a lad, on returning to port the first time after rounding the Horn, and known the exhilaration of the trade winds.

The sixteen-foot salmon boat passed by the Hurley-burlies uncovering in the lapsing water, their black edges ripping white; it passed the checkered Pulling buoy floundering in the hollow swirl of waters; but still the old man was away in thought and fancy. Only when a salmon leapt out of a wave not fifty yards from the boat, followed by a big, black object, and at the shout of "'Errin' 'og!" from one of the rowers, did his eyes focus upon the moment, to see the porpoise rolling up and down again, like a great blubbered bottle. There were others, farther off.

"Tidden right to allow them, I say," said one of the rowers. "There be several on'm! They'm taking of the fish, you know, all the time. If the water-baillies would do some work with a rifle out yurr sometimes there'd be some sense to it."

There was a school of porpoises. They had followed a run of salmon from the Lundy Race, a dozen miles and more westward from the bar. Several salmon leapt to escape the predacious mammals, each of which would tear away its bite from a fish, then pursue another. They were hunting not from hunger but for sport. The sight of many dark shapes rolling up and under again filled each man with hatred. The sweeps ceased to ply, as they watched. It seemed that there were at least a dozen porpoises in the school. Another rolled up just behind the stern of the boat. In its mouth was pink flesh, and a glint of silvery scales, together with the fin torn from near the salmon's vent. In his anger Old Masts-and-Yards spat at it, squirting brown tobacco juice at it, his only weapon of offence. When his anger had gone, he said:

"There be fish about, so pull hard, lads. They'm running! I never seed so many leaping like this all my born days."

Whistling Paddy hissed with excitement.

7

The boat went down towards a spit of sand on which gulls, white in the sunshine rushing before and after the shadows of clouds, were perched head to wind. The starboard sweep was eased, the sandbank grew nearer. When with a slight bump the keel-shoe grazed the sand, Whistling Paddy jumped out and a coil of rope was flung to him. Winding the end round his waist, he shoved out the boat again, and at once it was rowed with long strong pulls into the current. The old man paid out the rope over the stern, and then the net followed, the dark two hundred yards of it, eight feet deep, corked along its head rope and leaded at the heel. The heel rope sank away immediately, leaving the corks on the choppy surface to hold the net vertical.

The cast was made on the shape of a horseshoe, and by the time all of the net had dropped over the stern the ankle boots of Whistling Paddy leaning back on the rope were sunken in wet sand beyond their tops. He tugged them free, and with all his strength began to plod along the water line towards the boat which, having come round its loop against the tide, had touched into the bank again. The three men clambered out; one ran to join Whistling Paddy, whose head was bowed, for the pull of the tide on the net was almost beyond his strength.

The second man bent the dark and dripping net over his shoulder, and together they slowly plodded towards the other pair, likewise hauling. When about thirty paces apart they stopped, and began to pull hand under hand, slowly; short slow pulls against the weight of water which had crushed the horseshoe shape and borne the seine past the idle boat.

Minute after minute the four men hauled unspeaking, two at the head rope, two at the heel rope. The dull morning grew lighter; the waves were washed with tinny sunlight. The porpoises were now around the distant bar buoy. As the distorted arc of the corks was drawn imperceptibly small, hauling was easier. When only the purse remained in the sea the bodies of the men were bent forward and they hauled rapidly, the net falling at their feet, while their eyes stared for sight of fish.

The purse, drawn in fast, was empty except for green crabs and stones with bladder weed growing on them.

No word was spoken. The youngest man ran away to the boat and started to pull it to the piled net. His mate ran to help him. "They 'errin' 'ogs've drove the fish out agen, I reckon." They walked the boat up in the shallow water. In the meantime the old man and his son, one at heel and t'other at head rope, were shaking the net free of stone and crab—crushing crabs underfoot—and piling the net on the sand, preparatory to repiling it upon the boat's stern. Afterwards a rest of a couple of minutes while they gazed seawards for sign of jumping fish. Nothing: but the press of the tide was lessening, and at a word from the skipper a second draught was shot.

Once again the shedding of the net; the full-strenth pulling on the heavy sweeps; the slow plodding haul from the sandbank; the emerging after twenty minutes of the

purse; again only crabs and seaweed and insignificent flat
fish shaken free. No cursing of luck after the vain fatigue of
labour which made the backs of the recently unemployed
men, unused to such work, painful to straighten again.
Again the youngest went for the boat; again the piling and
repiling of the net; and when the third draught was shot
and hauled in, as before, the tide was slack and almost at
once began to flow.

Wind was freshening, flinging afar sprays from the tops
of combers before they curled and plunged in bounding
white turmoil upon the hidden shoals of the bar. The tide
began to move in faster, creeping up the sandbank. A large
bird flew with powerful thrusts of wings up the estuary,
settling with a splash beside the Pulling buoy.

"He knows where th' vish be, I reckon," said one of the
amateur netsmen. The skipper did not reply.

He was afraid of shoaling water. White water was death
to all deep-water sailors. So the salmon boat left the bank
for the lighthouse shore, where the fourth draught of the
day was shot. The porpoises were seen nearer in the fairway, heading for the place the boat had left. One of the
new men grumbled. He glanced, as he hauled, now and
again at the black bird near the pulling buoy. Tipping up
and disappearing underwater, and swimming with rapid
thrusts of its webbed feet, the shag caught two codling and
a sea-trout, returning to the surface with each fish to tip it
head first into its hooked beak before gulping it down.
After each swallowing, and before the succeeding tip-up
and dive, its small emerald eye stared at the men, its
enemies, across the widening gulf of water.

"There be fish over yonder," said the youngest man to
his mate.

"Don't waste your breath, lad; save it for hauling," said
the skipper.

"I could've made more on th' dole this last month, had I
known it," replied the other.

A fish leapt inside the arc of the corks. A big 'un! In silent intentness the purse of the net was drawn in, and there was the salmon, threshing upon the watery shingle. Steady, lad! Whistling Paddy got his hand round the wrist of the fish by the tail and, securing his grip, lifted it sinuating up the shingle, where he dropped it to thump it on the base of the skull with a sodden length of driftwood.

"Fifteen pun, I reckon, Father!"

Fifteen pounds at two shillings a pound from Julius Caesar, who collected fish for the lorry which came from Bristol to meet every tide. Thirty shillings. That was something, but they would have to take many more fish before the licence and wear of boat and net was paid for, let alone their living.

After another draught there was danger of the tide taking the net among the rocks lying off the shingle shore; so they rowed up-tide to the Shrarshook ridge. They rowed hard to get into the fairway. The tide was tumbling over the low rocks, but they reached the Pulling buoy in safety, and from there approached rapidly the lower end of the bank. Behind them, between ridge and lighthouse, the tide was leaping and pouring. On a rock raised above the others squatted the black bird, with wings half spread and a fish-tail sticking out of its gullet. It moved its swings at the elbows, in order to shake down into its crop the live eel which was trying to writhe a way out of the scalding juices of the crop, past a flatfish and a small bass, both inert but still breathing. The shag's crop was gorged; the outheld wings eased the weight.

"That bliddy bird picks up a livin' easy," complained the youngest man. "The bliddy thing ought to be shot."

8

There was no need to do more than paddle in the fairway, to keep control of the boat, with the tide flowing fast. There was time for one more draught only. Amid the chop

of wavelets that broke irregularly with foamy tops, with
bubbles rushing under, the open boat glided past the de-
creasing extent of the Shrarshook at five knots. The
wooden props which shored the barges, while gravel had
been dug and shovelled on board at low tide, had been
taken aboard the squat tarred vessels. Frothy flumes of
water were pouring into the pits beside the barges, rocking
the matchsticks flung away by the men at work, as they
had lit their fags. Now the gravel-diggers were resting.
Smoke wandered from galley chimneys.

A heron flew across the Pool with heavy hollow flight,
making for the duckponds in the marshes behind the sea-
wall.

"One more draught, lads; the tide be makin' fast."

They shot the draught, while other boats coming in
from the bar passed over their floating corks. The salmon
boats swept by, making for the backwash or eddy which
lay off the curve of the sea-wall. It was hard work hauling
in the net against the pull of the tide; and underwater the
heel rope was carried against the big rocks on the bed of the
Pool. The net was hung up; it had to be pulled free, for
now time was against the crew. As they hauled, it was seen
that at least half a dozen salmon were on the right side of the
corks. The fish drove about to find a way out of the net;
their back fins reamed along the top of the water and
caused some excitement among the two amateur
fishermen. Visions of much money at the week-end made
their eyes keen; but the skipper and his son, whom the seas
had taught patience, hauled stoically as before. One fish
rushed unseen towards the edge of the gravel, turning in a
great boil of sand and water and sped back, the sounds of
its acceleration being just audible as drumming or thrud-
dling through the noises of pouring water. It was a big
sea-trout.

They hauled in; but when the seine came into near
water, and finally upon the gravel, it was empty, a hole
torn in the purse. Then the skipper dropped his rope and,

raising his fist to the sky, began to curse the water-baillies for not dredgin' up they flamin' hellerin' rocks instead of tryin' to stop honest men arter a lifetime o' work on the high seas from keepin' out o' the' Grubber (workhouse or poor-house) by turnin' an honest penny! They dalled blasphemin' Board Boogers mocked Holy Writ, and they water-baillies were disciples o' Satan Hisself!

His words were heard by Julius Caesar, skipper of another boat, as it moved past the ridge.

"Takin the Holy Book's name in vain won't never pay you, midear!" came the warning from the bulky solemn-faced man. "You watch what you'm about, you a Masts-and-Yards man and all; you ought to knaw better than take the Book's words in vain!"

"Go and caulk yourself, you psalm-singing hellfire trader of a bliddy boy, you longshore beachcombin' son o' a ship's cat!"

Julius Caesar was a mere fifty years of age; thirty years younger than Masts-and-Yards.

"You should knaw better at your age than to talk like that, midear,' called back the other, from his boat rapidly receding. The current took it past the Pool buoy leaning at a steep angle upstream, a plume of water flung over its top. "Aiy, you should knaw better, old man, God is not mocked!" came over the water.

The stentorian tones had been heard by several of the crews of the gravel barges, waiting on the Shrarshook for the tide to float them off and take them up to the ports of Bideford and Barnstaple. Some men, looking on, laughed with derision. Because of his known hardness for money, Julius Caesar was not popular; but he thought they derided, not himself or his manner, but the Word. So he felt he was fighting the Good Fight.

Old Masts-and-Yards growled and spat as he repiled the torn net, muttering to himself about a local praicher who had nivver been beyond shoaling water. The younger men, the ex-soldiers, were amused and superior, winking to one another at the nonsense of old men, both so daft as each other. But even they, sceptical of so much since their return home from the war, were quietened when, only a little more than twelve hours later, they recalled the preacher's words.

The Crake came again in the darkness; this time with Death.

9

Towards midnight old Masts-and-Yards got out of bed, where he had been sleeping partly clothed, awoke his son, and went downstairs in his socks. After a cup of strong hot tea and some bread and beef-dripping, the two put on several extra garments, all frayed and worn—jersey, waistcoat, trousers, jacket—which had been hanging to dry on a line across the ceiling. Clad thus against the cold night air, they left Irsha Court, each carrying a sweep, which had been brought up from the boat during the afternoon tide lest they be stolen.

Tiny bluish-yellow jets of gas-light marked the sett-stoned streets and broad quay, beside which black masts and rigging of coastal craft arose among the stars. The night was almost silent, with faint slappings and murmurs of the ebb on boat and mooring and wet step of slip. On the farther shore lights shone in unseen houses, their thin reflections wriggling like golden eels beyond shapes of darkest shadow which were the moored salmon boats.

Father and son, unspeaking, waited by a bollard, to which the rope of a quayside ketch was made fast. At last voices were heard. A red spark came nearer, with the sounds of shuffling soft footfalls of boots worn to the uppers.

Without a word the four men went down the wet stone slip to the rocks and sand; hauled in their boat by the dripping painter; then away down on the ebb, by the spinning sea-top of the Pool buoy; and so to the dark rising ridge of the Shrarshook, now musical with the cries of wading birds. At steady intervals the roving beam of the lighthouse caressed the boat, and lit in a frail flash the outlines of gravel barges anchored there for the tidal shift.

There was money to be made in gravel during the immediate post-war years. Government subsidies to builders for new houses were £260 a house, and many an ugly little square building was going up, built by men who were one-man builders, masons seizing their chance to get on and make money. Gravel, sharp Two Rivers gravel, after washing in fresh water to remove the salt, made the best mortar.

Hoarse human tones came from the water-lapped dark of the Shrarshook, followed by the thud of wood baulks and the crush of boots on wet shell fragments and stone, as sleepy men jumped after the props to shore upright their barges. A blot of intense light swept over the ridge, stared blindingly a moment on the dark scene, blinked into darkness, and leapt again into seaward shine of vigilance clear and unfaltering for some seconds. Distantly came the roar of waves on the bar.

The two men dipped the sweeps, to keep steering way on the boat. Flashes of phosphorescence glimmered green and died in every placid swirl left by the blades. Old Masts-and-Yards and his son sat aft, the piled seine between them. In silence the boat glided away, leaving behind the ridge and the lonely lighthouse among the sandhills. Past the Pulling buoy, writhing heavily ahead of the racing troughs and crests of the tide on the rocks, the dreaded Hurleyburlies, and down the fairway to the loose sandbank near the South Tail. The water flickered with pale-green lights of phosphoric plankton, minute life of the summer sea.

There was little wind, the air was heavy with moisture, and rain began to fall as they were shooting the first draught. At first a soft drizzle, then a steady suent wetness which laid the thin clothes of the ex-service men against their bodies. They did not mind being wet; their minds held memories of hopeless cold nights and days in the flooded winter crater-zones of Somme and Ypres which kept them fortified, in that they thought of the roof over their heads when they should return, where they were safe, secure, where they could be warm, and to which they might go and come at will. So they toiled without loss of spirit in darkness that might have been water, except that it could be breathed.

After slow heaving, they heard something in the purse, and, pulling in the net, were disappointed to find within, threshing and flacking, squat fish with thin rasping tails and heavy angular bodies nearly flat.

"Thorn-backs!" one man cried in disgust.

Whistling Paddy sought a Swedish knife from his pocket, flicked open the single blade, and stabbed the two great fish many times, to sever the spinal cords. They were skate. On their backs were bony talons. They shone palely as they were lifted up, to be slithered into the well of the boat. Of little value, parts of the fish were used in the fish-and-chip shop, poor men's food.

The crew waited for the ebb to slacken. When the tide was low, the skipper shot another draught, but instead of rowing round and hauling in directly, he told the two men at the sweeps to linger in the fairway, with the net gently bellied by the tide just on the make. This was illegal; it prevented fish from ascending, the net became a 'fixed engine for the taking of salmon', thus, in both theory and practice, stopping fish from reaching the nets higher up.

The salmon either were not running or were remaining over the bar, afraid of the porpoises which had been seen several times during the day. Some of them had gone up with the previous tide almost to the towns' bridges. At any rate, the net was empty.

The skipper shot one more draught; then he left, afraid

of shoaling water, even mindful of the dreadful menace of white water.

The boat went up to the next place. Here they took two salmon, and were jubilant: two grilse, of only about nine pounds, but they were *fish*, and made three that day!

"There be a school comin' in, I reckon," said one of the men. They hastened to shake out the net, for the skipper said that they would bestways cast from the lower end of the ridge. There were no loose rocks in the fairway at that place. It had taken him and his son three hours to repair the torn purse.

10

It was from the lower end of the Shrarshook that the last draught of the little company of four was shot, before the boat was burned. The tragic circumstances of that final draught were discussed for many weeks, even months, afterwards. While Whistling Paddy held the rope on the ridge, his figure silhouetted now and again by the sweeping beams of the lighthouse, the boat pulled across the tide, while being carried aslant the drift of water. It was turning round in a wide arc amidst its own wake of phosphorescence, the rowers straining at the sweeps to bring the boat back quickly to the ridge, when a big salmon, thought to be all of forty pounds, leapt from the water and fell with a splash only a few feet away from the skipper in the stern. As he called to the rowing men to bend their backs a hissing noise accompanied by a tremendous downpour made him peer into the gloom.

"Keep you a-going lads, keep you a-going!" he called out.

Almost immediately afterwards a scream, strange and plaintive, seemed to be coming from the agitated water beside the boat. The upheaval was so severe that the boat was violently rocked. Water poured over the starboard gunwale. One of the rowers lost his sweep, and fell over backwards; the other swore in his fear.

"Keep you a-going lads!" said the skipper.

A dim white patch arose out of the murk. The sea became lashed with foam, filled with green flecks of fire, and the moaning scream came again, arising out of the turmoil, and filling all with terror.

Others heard the noise. There was a shout from way up the ridge—"The Crake!"

Whistling Paddy on shore was yelling. His words were indistinct, but it was thought he cried that he was not able to hold the rope. At the same time the net was being hauled off the stern-sheets of the boat by something big in the water. Seeing what was happening, one of the rowers clambered aft and grabbed the rope coiled under the remaining bulk of the net, now leaping off the boat into the water.

The old man began to curse him. "Get you back to the thole-pins, you loobey, or I'll have 'ee in irons afore us be finished!"

The younger man took no notice, as he took a couple of turns of rope round his sweep.

"Don't get the wind up, Dad," he said. "Us wull lose the net else. 'Tes a school of mullet; I seen 'em in Cork Harbour in bliddy thousands."

"Leave me to mind th' net! Git you back to the sweep, you g'rt fool, you!" cried the skipper.

The man had hardly got back to his thwart when the cries on shore changed into yelps of distress.

"I can't hold'n no longer, I can't hold'n, Feyther," came Paddy's voice faintly.

"All right, boy, us be comin'; keep you a-goin!" cried the old man.

The rope-end in the boat was still turned round the handle of the sweep. The boat was drifting fast with the tide, though seemingly still. The man who held the sweep placed it between the oaken pins and braced himself to hold it there, for the rope was now snaking over the gunwale, giving little leaps and slashing the surface of the water. He braced himself for the tug to come. The skipper was by now without speech; he had no power left to compel the mutinous man to do his bidding, to row ashore to help his boy, whom he already saw, in a moment of insight, as lost. A deep-water man, a masts-and-yards sailor for fifty years, he knew what the spouting of water portended; he had seen monsters of the deep ocean main; but in his very experience, by his knowledge of the ways of God upon the face of the waters, he was helpless; for only the old knew the truth, and nobody listened to an old'n.

When the rope had run out of the boat the jerk on its beam was so heavy that it almost capsized. Then the boat was being turned about as it was pulled sideways, its gunwale almost under water.

"Loose the rope end, loose it, you sod!" cried the other man.

His mate responded by tipping up the sweep so that it slid overboard. The boat was now free.

Other shouts were coming from the darkness. The cries of Whistling Paddy had ceased.

When the old man found his voice he called out, "Be ee all right, Paddy boy?" and when there was no reply he stood up, took the other sweep, and, putting it over the stern, began to scull towards the ridge, working it to and fro with a rolling motion.

The two men sat still on the thwarts, and the bump into the shore of the Shrarshook, near the barges now waiting to go home on the tide after the night's work, flung them on their backs among the cold and slippery skates.

Old Masts-and-Yards walked down the ridge, calling to his son. There was no answer. A hailing voice from beyond the barges cried out that there was something beating about in the Pool. Another voice was heard, "'Tes

the vengeance of the Lord come among sinners; 'tes the
Lord's wrath come among us!" It was the voice of Julius
Caesar.

The old man went down the length of the Shrarshook,
calling the name of his son. The two men stood dejectedly
by the boat. The net was gone; there would be no seeing
that again. They would have to find other work. Rain was
falling lightly; the rotating beam of the lighthouse was an
opaque blur.

11

From the quay across the water one or two women, who
had heard the shouting, and thought it might be trouble
with the water-bailiffs, watched in the darkness. The
mournful hail of old Masts-and-Yards came over the
water. As the onlookers waited, they saw an insignificant
light burning upon the ridge; they watched it wavering
about like a will-o'-the-wisp, before it fell and died out.

"Oh, my Gor, what be that, midear? Did 'ee zee'n,
surenuff?"

"'Tes trouble I shouldn't wonder, maybe 'tes they
water-baillies."

The flare had been burned by Julius Caesar, whose
practice it was to enwrap himself with newspapers at night
under his jersey, as a protection against cold. Now, like a
picture prophet of old, except for his bulk and girth, which
certainly did not accord with any fasting in the wilderness,
he was advancing down the southern shore of the
Shrarshook, bearing aloft a torch of rolled newspapers in
one hand, while with the other he pulled more paper from
around his middle.

"Brothers!" he chanted to the night, out of a feeling of
self-justified joy. "Brothers, fellow sinners all, the wages
of sin is death, and 'e what taketh the Lord's name in vain

shall be in danger of hivverlastin' 'ell fire." He waved the burning newspapers.

Other boats were appearing on the water-line of the ridge. One was rowing hard against the tide, a man in the bows standing up and looking for sign of floating corks. Men gathered round Julius Caesar. The feeble flare, with an occasional spark fleeting down towards the coppery crescent moon low in the vapours of the west, revealed their quiet faces. Stealthily the water crept up the sloping bank. From the direction of the lighthouse came a rushing roar as the sea poured into the rocky pools and lagoons below the shingle shore. The men discussed what had happened.

The net had been torn away from the boat, that was certain. As for Paddy on shore, the rope enwound about his middle and over his shoulder, and held by a half hitch— as was his habit—had pulled him into the water. The boat crew at the top of the ridge had heard his feeble cries in the water, following a great shower of spray, and the slashing plunge of some fish or animal.

"'Tes no use for to strive with a man's reason," intoned Julius Caesar. "What be the Lord's hidden purpose, no man can dispoot. 'Tes the Crake come agen, for to warn sinful men, hanimated by their own pride, which goeth before a fall, for to teach us, sinners all, to live humbly in the ways o' the' Lord."

"Put a sock in it," muttered one of the ex-service men; but the words were unheard in the general response of "Amen".

12

Boats searched, in the chill light of the descendant moon, up the courses of the Two Rivers until dawn, looking for floating corks which would reveal the net. They had little hope of finding the missing man alive; they searched as an act of reverence to themselves, and to their neighbours, to bring the body home, for the churchyard. That was the natural place of a man when he was cut off, to be laid to rest in the place where he was born, where there was love for him, surely, lingering in the stones he had known, in the faces of friends and comrades, and most of all in the heart of his father.

That is how it seemed to me, when I learned the story of Masts-and-Yards, and found out why, so often, in sunny weather and rainy times too he was to be seen by the War Memorial. Had not all his sons been lost at sea? His neighbours knew it, and so they searched for the boy Paddy, to bring him home to his father.

The boats which searched until dawn found nothing. One volunteer crew kept a look-out during the ebb, but saw nothing of the net. The mystery remained for another day; and as has been said, provided the only real topic of talk in the village, and its seventeen taverns and inns, until the matter became clear the following morning.

The pilot of the Lundy boat *Lerina*, going out top of the tide, saw something floating near the bar buoy. Standing in nearer, he saw what were apparently the corks of the missing net. The ropes were twisted round the chain to which the buoy was anchored. The *Lerina* heaved to, and a boat hook caught the head rope. Hauling part of the net aboard, they recovered the body of Whistling Paddy, distended with water. It was even as had been said: the rope was made fast to his chest by two turns secured by a half hitch. It was drawn tight, confirming the belief that he had been pulled at a considerable pace through the water.

The *Lerina* turned back, to where on the quay a stretcher on wheels was waiting: for the boat had been watched from the lighthouse, the keeper of which had telephoned to the police in the village and to the doctor.

The body, covered by a canvas, was taken off in the rowing boat, after which the Lundy packet, prepared to encounter the formidable tide sweeping down the Irish Sea into the open Atlantic, set her sails to aid the efforts of the oil engine which drove the screw.

On her way across Bideford Bay the captain of the *Lerina* saw ahead a school of porpoises. They were not rolling and leaping through the sea in the usual manner of herring-hogs; indeed, when the captain of the *Lerina* looked through his glass he saw that one was jumping in the manner of a salmon trying to escape the pursuit of seal or porpoise. The porpoises, about a score of them, were appearing in all directions, quite unlike a school following a leader in a drive after food. The porpoises were being pursued.

Suddenly he saw what was after them. An immense shape arose out of the water, a little whale, which opened its wide mouth, set with teeth like tent-pegs, to snap at, but to miss, its prey, before diving down again and showing a fluked tail as it disappeared.

The *Lerina* kept on her course, which would cross that of the line of porpoises. The next time the monster appeared, it was with a porpoise being champed in its jaws, which were red with blood. The killer's head was blunt, shining smooth and black, with two patches of white above and behind its two small eyes. From a spiracle in the top of the head a jet of vaporous water rose hissing. It was a killer whale, a carnivorous animal which fed on flesh and fish alike. In companies the killers sometimes attacked the largest sperm whales, springing at the vast flippers to tear away flesh with chop of jaws able to crush seal or man with equal ease. *Orca Gladiator*, the grampus . . .

So that was the origin of the Crake! Well, not exactly the origin, for the screaming cries in the night had probably been made by a seal in its death agonies. The grampus had followed the porpoises and seals up the estuary, themselves following the runs of salmon, and, coming up against the net, had simply carried it away. Such was its weight that, had it chanced to arise under a sixteen-foot salmon boat, it could have overturned it and scarcely been checked in its movement through air and water.

Whistling Paddy was buried by the Vicar, himself an old naval chaplain, with traditional ritual and discipline. The net was recovered, torn in the middle, and burned; so was the boat. Old Masts-and-Yards continued to live in Irsha Court. And the last time I saw him was as the first: he was standing in the sunshine by the War Memorial.

I knew then that he was there to be near his sons. In his thoughts he saw them, and talked to them; they were all ages to him, from small children to grown youths. He told their ghosts about the youngest, little Paddy; he saw their mother with them, too, she who had died when they were children, so that they were brought up, while he was away for months at a time, sailing the deep waters of the seven seas, by a sister of his, who now lay in the churchyard. One day they would all be together again; the good Book said so. He had always believed it to be true, although he had never wanted any man, certainly not one like Julius Caesar, to tell him so.

Until they should all meet again, there was work to be done.

"A man must splice a rope," he said, and now I understood the meaning, the experience, behind the simple phrase. This man had lived by courage all his life in the perils of the sea; and until his own final dissolution he would continue that way.

A HERO OF THE SANDS

A dog fight is always stimulating, usually interesting, occasionally amusing, rarely dangerous. Once on the summer sands, in the glorious days of wearing a beard, no shirt, trousers tied up with string, and shoes without socks, I came upon a very funny scene. There before me was a Pekinese dog, hanging to the lower part of one section of a visitor's trousers! I was prepared to enjoy myself to the full for the sight the gods had provided, when my mood of detached amusement changed. The action looked to be complicated; for while the embarrassed fellow was trying to knock away the little beast with a newspaper, a big Alsatian wolfhound loped over to see what was doing and, picking up the Pekinese, proceeded to shake it.

The visitor, a mild-looking man, realized that, being British, he would have to be a hero, as only women and children were near—myself remaining conveniently aloof, as all objective artists should be. Accordingly he grabbed the hindlegs of the wolfhound, which, thus suspended, continued to shake the Pekinese until the little dog dropped off.

And then, suddenly, a situation of the gravest peril! There the fellow was, holding the great snarling brute by the hindlegs, fortunately with its back towards his front, while his arms sagged gradually and the jaws of the angry animal clashed nearer and nearer his knees. And while he was thus engaged, the Pekinese, fluff-snuffling up behind him, retook its hold on his trousers. What could the hero do?

What could *I*, no hero, do? I hitched up my trousers, and tying the string tighter round my middle, prepared for action. Swallowing the saliva in my mouth, I advanced upon the struggle. I felt courage coming into my stomach, empty but for a rind of stale cheese and an old piece of bread—food, in those days, was generally scorned as an unspiritual thing.

Meanwhile the real hero had walked into the sea. The Alsatian, no hydrophile, quit at the first breaker, but the Pekinese was nearly drowned before it let go. Bravo! I thought: he is another Solomon. I was wrong. Hardly had the hero waded on shore again, than he was attacked by an hysterical woman who was nursing the Pekinese in her arms. Solomon then proceeded to get it back from both plaintiffs at once; for while the Pekinese owner was describing him to himself in terms of herself, the owner of the wolfhound was shouting at him: (*a*) it was a valuable animal he had been injuring, (*b*) it was not British to be cruel to animals, and (*c*) he deserved flogging.

That night in the pub in the village up the valley, kept by Charley, himself a very tough customer on occasion, I heard the hero, over his fourth glass of whisky, explaining the ironies of his predicament that morning; for the Pekinese, apparently, belonged to his mother-in-law.

"Ah, there's all sorts about nowadays," remarked Charley noncommittally, as he leaned over the bar beside his pint of beer and rum, and spat past a customer's ear into a cuspidor placed on the lime-ash floor.

After a while the visitor asked about the heads of animals on the wall behind the bar. There were four of them, close together, greasy-looking objects stained by years of fug and tobacco smoke. Fixed to a piece of wood by the neck, the dead and stuffed existed among various knives. Two of the heads had once belonged to badgers. A year or two back Charley used to go badger-digging with his famous terrier, the Mad Mullah. The other two were un-British.

"That's him, that's the Mullah," remarked Charley, pointing at the dingy old dog sniffing at the visitor's trousers. "Get away, Mullah!"

The old dog took no notice, but continued to sniff without emotion and almost without movement.

"He's old now, the Mullah," went on Charley musingly. "He don't take the slightest notice of what I tells him. He's slow, and don't care no more, see? But when 'e 'ad 'is teeth, Mullah'd tackle the biggest boar badger, and when once he'd got a holt o' any brock Mullah'd hang on. Aye, he'd hang on for a pastime! Not like other terriers, all barking and fuss, but well away from a badger, noomye' Mullah'd be right up, facing the badger, yesmye!"

"Would he ever fight other dogs in the village?" enquired that morning's hero of the sands.

"Not unless another dog tackled'n first," replied Charley. "But no dog would interfere with the Mullah in they days, they knew'n too well, see."

As so often happens, dog and master seemed to share the same temperament. Both were undemonstrative, loyal, easy-going, but awkward customers if roused. And yet (such is the paradox of life on occasion) I was to observe, on the following morning, certain behaviour of Charley and his dog in the street outside my cottage which was contrary to what I had observed about him heretofore.

2

There was a guant, somewhat argumentative and awkward old farmer who lived opposite my cottage, nicknamed 'Stroyle' George. He was going downhill. He had only his grown-up daughter to help him; his rented arable fields were foul with weed, particularly of cough grass, locally called stroyle.

As Charley was walking down the street, with the old terrier Mad Mullah, 'Stroyle' George came out of his yard followed by Roy, his cattle-dog. Roy was a timid dog, afraid of lightning and thunder. I had observed this recently, during a sudden storm. "The rain came down like aught out of a sieve," 'Stroyle' George had said to me, "and the bliddy dog cleared at the first clap." 'Stroyle' George usually spoke as he ploughed; he drove the straighest of furrows, he was a master worker; but his argumentative tongue, working so hard against the irregularities of others, had been his ruin. He thought too much. His speech was simple, direct, and with the least use of words. Thus, cantankerous and poor, he spent most of his time arguing, protesting, declaiming against the obvious faults and deficiencies of others. And, since men impose on their dog or dogs, Roy was a bit of a nervous wreck.

When I saw the farmer and the publican approaching one another, and the farmer's dog dodging behind his master when it saw the Mad Mullah, I got up from my desk and watched from the window, for it looked to be interesting.

Roy, the timid but handsome cattle-dog, had been afraid of the Mullah for several years. Shouted at by his master since puppy-hood, Roy was usually hysterically responsive to a friendly word. He was uncertain, afraid of his neighbours. Roy's mother had been the same; she was the successor to an old dog which 'Stroyle' George had shot, and the bitch had witnessed the shooting. She appeared to me to have a semi-human intelligence; she used to send waves of semi-human appeal to me with her eyes as she showed her teeth in nervous grins and wriggled her belly on the ground, often rolling over before me in subjection. Many of her puppies, of mixed breed, had been drowned. Eventually 'Stroyle' George gave her away, keeping one of her dog pups, who grew up to be the handsome Roy, afraid of lightning, thunder, the report of a gun, and many other things, including the Mad Mullah.

Nowadays, the Mullah, slow and aged, was as inoffensive as he was independent. He lay about in the road, scratching and biting his coat, sleeping on his side in the sun. Wheels of passing motorcars whizzed a few inches from his head; he did not trouble. Sometimes a car, hooting and with squealing brakes, stopped just short of him, when the Mullah would raise his grey scarred head, give a glance, sigh, and settle down to sleep again. "He'll be runned over one day,"Charley used to explain. "I've told 'n again and again not to lie in the road, but he goes his own way. I can't help it. It makes no odds what I tells him, he don't trouble." Both man and terrier went their own ways, both were fearless and independent; they shared the same spirit, accepted the same world, the same kind of living. Charley may have thought that he took the Mullah for a walk on fine mornings; but it might have been that the Mullah was taking Charley for a walk, for the sake of old times. That is how it appeared to me, as the two shuffled down the street, looking slowly about them, each sufficient to himself. On this morning Charley carried his old muzzle-loader, for he was going to try for a rabbit on a little splat of land he had recently bought.

As they came down the street the yard-door of Hole Farm opened and 'Stroyle' George came out, Roy prancing around the near-ragged figure of his master. Then Roy, aware of the Mullah, slipped with wolf-like lope behind Charley and let out a sharp querulous bark.

The Mullah turned and looked at Roy over his shoulder. Roy, still loping, ran round again behind his master. The Mullah trotted after him slowly, but straight at him. Roy started to lope away, glancing back fearfully at the older dog following him slowly. Round and round the two men the almost leisurely procession went, until Roy, with another sudden sharp bark, turned and gripped the Mullah across the neck and shook him slightly.

"A-ah!" cried 'Stroyle' George. "Roy! A-ah you!"

With a nervous glance at his master, Roy began to lope around his wide orbit again. The Mullah followed, quietly, almost leisurely.

"He's got no teeth, you know," said Charley, surprisingly gentle, to the other man. "He can't do naught, but he's game—yesmye, he's game!"

"A-ah, you heller!" growled 'Stroyle' George, for Roy had turned and gripped the Mullah across the neck again, and worried him a moment before turning away.

As before, the Mullah followed the big cattle-dog.

"He won't leave him now," remarked Charley, in his reedy, conversational voice. "The Mullah fights for a pastime, you see. One day he'll be killed—he's got no teeth, you see. I tells him so often, but he don't trouble, noomye!" Charley spat, to disclaim further responsibility.

Round and round the two men went the slow lope-and-trot, Roy glancing first at his master then at the old terrier.

"Roy don't want to fight, you know," said 'Stroyle' George. "He could kill 'n sure enough, and knoweth it; but he's a-feared, all the same."

Mullah bant afraid of nought," said Charley shortly. "Mullah! *Mullah!!* Come yurr, you bad old jack, you!" for the Mullah had rushed at Roy and nipped him in the loose skin below the eye. He lost his grip immediately, against toothless gums.

"Only brown stumps, you see," repeated Charley in his quiet little reedy voice. "No teeth, you know. One day he'll be killed. I knows it. I told'n, too. Mullah!"

The Mullah ignored his master. He was going to get Roy.

"Darn the dog!" shouted 'Stroyle' George. "ROY! A-ah, you boogerin' booger, you!"

There was Roy, after another light worry, followed by the Mullah, who, without expression on his grey scarred face, trotted after him as though he were going to look at an indifferent bone hidden some distance away.

Suddenly 'Stroyle' George roared out, "Git 'oom!"; and Roy, after a glance at the Mullah, got home—he slipped through the stream-hole in the wall above the culvert which took the stream beside Hole Farm.

"Mullah! MULLAH!!" yelled Charley, in his old

Cardiff-docks fishporter voice; but uselessly, for the terrier, heedless of his master, likewise vanished down the hole.

A minute later, having run on his long legs down the bed of the stream beside the farmhouse, through the orchard and so into the yard, Roy appeared on the stone wall higher up the lane, beside the swarf furze bush which had been trying to grow there for a score of years. Easily he leapt down and trotted to stand by his master.

A minute or so later the door of Hole Farm opened and the voice of the farmer's daughter yelled, "Git 'oom! Out of it, you mangy old flea bag!" and a broom was used to impel the Mullah over the threshold.

"Gordarn the girl!" cried 'Stroyle' George. "You've set one on t'other again!"

"I didn't know!" protested the daugher. "Mullah came sniffin' about the place, cockin's his leg in my dairy, and I ban't standing for that!" The door slammed.

The dogs were revolving once more. Roy's tail was between his legs, and his backward glance more frequent. He showed his teeth. His was the weak spirit goaded: like the spirit of a former timid, peace-loving villager who once lived in the cottage I was occupying now. Goaded, they said in the village, bullied by the policeman for months, suddenly the cobbler seized a bill-hook and killed his tormentor—to die of grief the night before he was to have been hanged. But who, in the orbit of pads and tails and hanging tongues, was goading who this fine morning? The Mullah, that old toothless badger-dog, was enjoying himself, by the light in his eyes; until abruptly he found himself on his back while the powerful jaws of the hysterical Roy were mumbling about his throat.

Did the Mullah's owner, well known for his rages at times, raise his gun and shoot Roy? Did he curse Roy, and Roy's owner? Charley had been a bold fighter with fists in his day. In his bar, too, he could use a rough tongue at times; liable to order you outside if he didn't like your face or if you put your foot on one of the benches within the dark little room. How would Charley react to the murder of his old pet? I was amazed to see that he remained in his detached, almost nonchalant posture, deliberately giving every freedom of action to the farmer, all side-whiskers and gaunt peering nose. 'Stroyle' George raised his stick, shouting at his dog; and Roy sprang back, still yelping hysterically, and ran once again down the stream-hole. Mullah slowly picked himself up, shook himself, then followed leisurely after the cattle-dog.

"I said it," remarked Charley, in his twittering-finch voice, addressing the sky, as he leaned an elbow on the wall. "Mullah won't give in."

"My dog won't always be so nervous of him, you know!"

Charley spat. "Well, I told'n. I can't do no more."

I waited, watching the furze bush. No shaggy dog appeared on the skyline.

The farmhouse door opened, a voice cried out, "Roy and Mullah have gone down the stream to Cryde sands, I reckon," and the door was slammed again.

"Well," said Charley, "Mullah'll be back when he comes," and after a few more amiable words with the farmer, he slung his gun on his shoulder and went back up the road, his morning walk over.

3

About an hour later Roy was seen trotting through Cryde village, and, a long way after him, came the Mullah. It is possible that Roy had forgotten the Mullah, or rather that the Mullah's image was now obscured behind Roy's mental pictures of sea-weed pools and cake-owning summer visitors. The moon was almost at the full, and the spring-tides left the rocky pools of Down End exposed for a long way at midday.

Now Roy, who was usually so faithful and vigilant to attend the farmer and his daughter, who waited to be of use for cows in the street outside the farm every day, occasionally deserted his watch and went down to the bay when the moon was full in summer. It was his habit then to attach himself to any party with bare legs and prawning nets and sandwiches, to keep with them faithfully for a couple of days or so, then to return after his holiday to the village. During such excursions I had sometimes watched Roy standing on the rocks, looking down with great interest at one or another of his temporary friends prodding with gaffs into clefts and holes and pushing nets under the sea-weed fringe of pools.

This must have been in his mind that day, for Roy was observed trotting through the barley field and across the sandy burrows beside the stream which eventually cut through a gap in the sandhills and splayed out upon the shore. Arriving there, Roy sniffed at the strong and varied scents in the jetsam of the tide-line, before starting to cross the shore in the direction of the black ridges of rocks below Down End. On his way there he crossed an intersting scent. Following this up and down the sands, at length he came to a diminutive dog being led by a stout woman.

"Grr-r! Get away, you brute!" cried the woman, and picked up the Pekinese. "Don't be upset by the nasty dog, Consuelo darling; Mummie won't let it hurt you. Grr-r! Go away at once, you horrid brute! The impertinence!"

The brute, however, was obviously attractive to Consuelo; and panting with excitement, she managed to scramble out of her barreline owner's arms. Galloping away, Consuelo reached the handsome Roy and then, turning her back to him, she stared at the sea in a provoking attitude.

Roy, however, had seen some prawners on the rocks. As though ridding his pads of the scents of the old world, he kicked up a certain amount of sand with his hind feet, and then loped away, followed by the galloping Pekinese dragging her lead, heedless of her owner's entreaties, through the wet delta of the stream in the sands. Roy's mind was set on lobsters and crabs, which terrified and therefore absorbed him; he made straight for the rocks.

As he was nearing the first ridge, having outrun the unattractive little dog, he heard a familiar sound, and turning round he saw the Pekinese being attacked by a big dog. Naturally Roy had to return to see what was happening; but the grey apparition of the Alsatian made him afraid, so that he ran backwards and forwards, shifting always to be behind the big dog, while yelping and making other hysterical noises.

Then the Mad Mullah, who had been following Roy's scent, appeared on the sands. He trotted towards the grey-hackled Alsatian as casually as though he were going into the kitchen of the Lower House for his dinner. Trotting directly up to the Alsatian, the Mullah bit the wolfhound in the loose skin of the jaws. At once the Alsatian flung the Pekinese away and, springing upon the Mullah, bit him in the shoulder and began to shake him. Neither dog made any sound, either of growling or yelping; both dogs were killers. The Alsatian worried the smaller terrier in the furious silence of killing.

Roy had been throwing up his head and uttering shrill howls, but the silence of the deadly struggle seemed to change hysteria into strength. With hackles raised he ran at the Alsatian and bit him across the neck. Several visitors were warily approaching, including the son-in-law of the owner of the Pekinese, yesterday's hero of the sands, who was being urged by his wife to do something. Mothers were exhorting their children to keep back. Two men dared to approach and to thwack the Alsatian with their children's spades, while one boy had already thrown in vain his friend's model yacht, while the friend was scooping up pailfuls of sand to throw at the dogs from afar.

"Go on, *do* something!" cried the owner of the Pekinese.

Roy seemed to be fighting silently, locked to the wolfhound's jaw. A power seemed to be upon him, for he swung the grey dog about as though it were no heavier than the Mullah.

One of the men who had vainly tried to stop the fight with a child's spade was the owner of the Alsatian. The fellow now appeared with his wife's sunshade, open, which he prodded and spun in the faces of the writhing dogs. All that happened was the sunshade got slightly buckled; but bravely he persisted, possibly seeing himself in the role of bullfighter, in a position of great danger; but to the onlookers he was merely funny, as he cavorted about, just this side of danger.

Like a wrestler Roy swung the wolfhound, trying to put his enemy on its back. The Mullah had no interest in the fight: he stood some distance away, with drooping head, shivering, as though dazed by the realization of what had happened to him. Grey and tired, he limped away homewards.

Meanwhile the hero who the day before had held up the Alsatian by its hindlegs now had got hold of those legs again, after shouting to the parasol-flutterer to get hold of the other dog by its hindlegs. The two dogs held grimly to their bites upon one another's neck-skin, as their legs were drawn out.

"Now," said the hero of the sands, "Will someone light a newspaper and just bring it near their noses, please."

This was done. Flames of *The Daily Wail* separated the heads; whereupon the Alsatian turned and ran away in great long determined strides towards the north side of the bay.

As for Roy, he was making friends with everyone, looking up into many human eyes and panting happily, a new four-legged hero of the sands.

4

"You wouldn't do what I told you, would you?" jeered
Charley to his dog blinking on the mat by the kitchen fire
that afternoon. "You thought you knew better, didn't
you, eh? And let me tell you again, you obstinate old toad
you, you'll get runned over if you continue to lie in the
road. And you leave Roy alone in the future, see?"

The Mullah swelled; and slowly he sighed. His wounds
were yellow with iodine.

The very next day he was lying in the road again, on his
side, and Charley was lounging against his doorpost,
when 'Stroyle' George came up with his cows, followed
by Roy. Charley noticed that Roy was making as if to
dodge behind the farmer when he saw the Mullah; he
watched him hesitate; then swiftly and silently, as the old
dog's head was raised, Roy bounded forward with feathery tail and lightly touched nose-to-nose with the Mullah.

The Mullah's head sank again; he swelled for a sigh of
contentment: and with a joyous bark Roy leapt around his
master. From first to last the behaviour of both men and
dogs had seemed to me to be wonderful.

INCIDENTS OF AN AFTERNOON'S WALK

This author's aim in writing has always been to re-create, or bring to life again on paper with print, the life around him as he has seen and heard it. Never merely to write a beautiful style, or to make a perfect form for its own sake. Here is the world—always with awareness that it is but one man's limited world—and here is that which is to be seen, heard, and occasionally to be smelled and tasted. Take it or leave it, that is up to the reader; the writer cannot do better than try to bring some of the life he has known to paper. As for the dialogue, or the way people speak—well, he tries to reproduce the manner of speaking, and the words. Sometimes fortune smiles on him: thus the following dialogue occurred in a Devon court of Summary Jurisdiction, and was reported in a local paper. Someone had summoned a nieghbour, suspected of getting rid of that someone's noisy dog.

Cross-examination of defendant by the plaintiff's solicitor:

"What did the dog die of?"

"'A died of a Vriday, zur."

"Yes, but how did he die?"

"On 'a's back, zur."

"Yes, but what made him die?"

"'A's heart gived out, zur."

"Yes, yes, but how did he come by his death?"

"'A didden come to it, zur, it came to be."

"Yes, yes, yes, my good man, but what was the complaint?"

"There wadden nivver no complaint, zur; the neighbours was all satisfied."

That, of course, is a gift. But such repartee and wit is not rare, if one listens at the right places. Local speaking is usually good because it arises directly off work or action. I have only to listen to a neighbour of mine, on this hilltop, to hear graphic English which derives from the living scenery of that energetic smallholder's world.

One afternoon, upon setting out for a walk, I saw in the sunken lane outside my gate a bramble-torn cap, covering the shaggy hair of my neighbour. He was speaking to another farmer on the subject of what the Ministry of Agriculture, reverting to language of Latin rootage, was beginning to call *Rodent Control*.

"Aiy, there be a lot of bliddy rats about the viels now. In a month or two, the boogers will be down in the barns and stacks. Hundred and thousands o' the bliddy things; why, t'other night I stood by the gate upalong and if one bliddy rat rinned over me boots, why, I tell 'ee midear, there was bliddy thousands! I kep still; I had me gun, too; I could have shut a score with each barrel, but I knew if I so much as kecked one of the boogers with me boot, t'others would have mobilized me.

"I'll tell 'ee, the government should do zomething 'bout rats. They'm all for taking your money, but what about ridding us of rats? Last winter I took ninety-three of the boogers one morning out of my gins tilled in one viel. Ninety-three! Then there was thousands of the bliddy critturs left in the rabbuts' buries. Aiy, thousands and thousands! Booger, I caught one and tarred it, a bliddy girt stag-rat, and I let'n go agen, hoping he'd drave the others. But still I couldn't keep no eggs or chickens or chicken food, they ate the bliddy lot. Fast as I'd trap a couple of hundred, the'd spring up agen. One night, I'll tell 'ee, midear, listen to this, I hear'd a bliddy great galloping about on the ceiling over me aid (head) and my missus zaid to me, It be like a cart and hoss passing overaid, whatever can it be, Jack. I zaid, 'Tis they bliddy rats up auver. I coudden get a wink of slape all night, back and 'vore the boggers was proper bliddy galloping, like a bliddy aerial durby it was up there. Aiy. But I'll tell 'ee what I did! I tilled a gin for the boogers, but coudden catch nought. One day, tho', I cornered one behind the cupboard, and a bliddy girt stag-rat 'twas, jimmering and chammering at me, clinging to the bliddy wall, just out of reach of my bliddy stick it was, and wan bliddy cat on the top of the cupboard, anither on the shelf, and a couple of bliddy dogs waiting below! I kept the booger pressed there agen the bliddy wall with me stick, I warn't going vor leave'n now I'd got'n, not if I stayed there all bliddy night, and the cat and the bliddy dogs biding there too. Missus fetched a long stick but the bliddy thing was bent, and wouldn't titch the stag-rat, which opened its mouth and showed its bliddy teeth to me, and jimmering and chammering it was, with the bliddy cats howling up above and the dogs a-roaring and a-bawling down below and me yelling at the missus to yett (heat) the bliddy poker in the vire, I'd burn the booger out if it wouldn't come out, cruelty or no cruelty. Of course I knowed if one of they inspectors for the abolition of cruelty to hanimals was to have comed along, I should have been in Town, but what about cruelty of the bliddy rats to me, unable to get a wink of slape with them tritting 'bout overhead like a bliddy hossrace? So missus yett up th' poker, and I pressed 'n into the rat, saying burn you booger, burn, and gor'darn! the withering thing burst into vlames and rinned down the wall and not a bliddy dog would titch it. Lucky the door was shut, else 'twould have rinned out and maybe set vire to me neighbour's ricks, for 'twas the selfsame bliddy rat I had tarred. I 'spose the ither rats had drove'n, because of the smell, and the booger had comed into my place. I tell 'ee, there's hundreds and thousands of rats in the viels today."

The ragged cap was lifted, and the shaggy scalp scraped by broken nails. Then the conversation or monologue continued in the same language, the trapper telling the identical story again, word for word, laugh for laugh, in the traditional Devon manner.

2

Having taken this in, I set out on my walk. I crossed several fields, climbing over stone-and-earth banks, always on the look-out for a bull, for it was cattle country. I followed a small runner, grown with watercress and brook-lime, which led eventually to a pond. This little bit of water was a favourite place to visit, for I was always hoping to see a trout there. Not to kill; but to feel it being alive.

The stream which fed the pond was hardly more than a trickle, scarcely more than a yard in width and six or seven inches deep; but it was pure water, eventually joining the stream passing through Cryde village which was reputed to hold the biggest fish in Devon, owing to its teeming insect life. (I ought to say that this was before the motorcar generally "opened up the place", with consequent increase of summer visitors and the stream's inevitable pollution.)

The little pond was triangular and silted. It lay in the corner of the field, holding a few thousand gallons dammed by the stone wall. The water worked a grist-mill in the farm behind the manor house three hundred paces below. It was a huant of moorfowl and other water-birds.

As I came down the slope of the field I saw a heron standing at its muddy edge. The tall grey bird flapped away when I was four or five gunshots distant.

Not that I carried a gun; but herons know the habits of men, and, taking no chances, are up and away, usually, when well out of range.

Seeing me, the heron jumped, its broad grey wings scooping the air; but it was caught by the wind as it tried to rise, and could make no headway; so it turned down the wind and was carried in a long glide over the next field, where it swung round again, and alighted among the rough grass clumps and thistles. I could see the head on the long neck held up anxiously to watch me away, when it would return to its feeding.

I jumped over the earth-and-stone hedge, to find out what it had been eating. The mud under the broken turf had been made arrowy by its feet, as the bird had stalked from the pond's apex to the deeper water by the stone dam. After every dozen steps it had turned to peer into the pond, and at these stances the mud was much trodden; the heron had taken many steps forward to snick its prey out of the water. What had attracted it? I could see nothing.

I sat down and waited. Wind ruffled the pond's surface; wavelets lapped the margin, erasing and silting the arrowy footmarks. Very soon from the direction of the wooden fender came a noise like a duck quietly calling her ducklings; but it was a dryer, more brittle noise. A similar cry came from the bank, and then another: a chorus broke out over the pond.

I saw a rat running along with a frog in its mouth. It went into a hole in the bank continuing the stone dam. There was a well-trodden track leading into this hole, two inches wide—the path of the rats. One of the colony must have come out as the heron flew up, and seeing a frog on the bank, picked it up.

Many frogs were now apparent in the pond. Most of them were bull-frogs, smaller than the females. The glitter of the sun and the lessening cold had excited them to begin the search and struggle for mates. All things in nature have their seasons, and the males usually await the females; it is so with the bull-frog, which finding a female, makes sure of her by climbing upon her broad back, and clinging there in the attitude of a jockey at the gallop. I was, all unsuspecting, to be on this afternoon a spectator of a mad, whirling, ranine romance and tragedy.

A female walked out of the water as I watched, and the

movement drew four unattached bull-frogs. She was mounted by the quickest, but carried him six inches only before the other frogs began to muscle in on his racket. I am sorry if this American slang phrase hurts the reader's susceptibilities, but I am no stylistic writer: I repeat, my aim is always to convey to the reader what my eyesight puts into my brain. The frogs were muscular creatures; they made a racket, or noise; they were competitive, pitiless, entirely selfish. The phrase therefore is used, although it belongs to the gangsters of the U.S.A. who have probably never heard of the little pond behind the hamlet of Putsborough in North Devon.

The jockey was prepared for musclers-in. With a slow but well-judged shove with his off-hind foot he laid one on its back. Then he croaked, as though trying to get his mount to start again. She carried him forward another three inches and stopped. He dug his hands deeper under her armpits, urging her on with calf and spur. She remained motionless. A rival greener than the jockey climbed leisurely up, avoiding the thrust of elastic hing-legs; and digging his arms in, the green rival bent his head forward and slowly arched his back, in an attempt to unseat the jocket. Their stifled croaking stirred to movement the three other frogs who had been squatting behind them. These would-be jockeys hopped forward, to receive immediate thrusts of feet in their faces. Two of them overturned. They got upright again, and squatted still, as though in oblivion.

The greener frog who had scrambled up was now trying to throttle the jockey. The three fingers and thumb of each hand were clenched with his striving. In other words, *he was muscling-in*.

For nearly a minute the muscling-in continued. Then the female decided to move; she took two heavy hops forward. The squeaky cries of the jockeys began again. The three also-rans moved after them. Two of them collided, and as though in despair one hopped astride the other. He was carried forward a few inches, but dismounted, and turned back. The movement of my foot had drawn him; he leapt at the toe of my shoe, fell off, and went back disconsolately towards the water, passing another aspirant who was hurrying forward, gay with a bit of weed round his neck.

Meanwhile the race was continuing. The steed was walking and hopping forward with her double load. During one of her pauses the fourth frog sprang, receiving from the green rival a quiet, sure kick in the throat which laid him out; but picking himself up, he tried again. The original jockey sat still, croaking weakly, vainly, for motion; but the green super-jockey, the line of whose back was now almost oval with the strain of throttling, kicked out again at a fresh aspirant, and missed. Immediately the aspirant gripped his leg and hung on, while the steed moved forward a few more paces. During the next interval the aspirant managed to grip the other leg of the green super-jockey, and stepping up on the wide haunches of the female, secured what may have given a satisfying illusion of superiority.

It was no longer a race; it was an omnibus. The omnibus progressed unevenly, with noises like the tooting of horns blown asthmatically. It had four pairs of protuberant headlights, the reflection of which glinted in the sun. It appeared to have been broken down completely, so I left it, having other business with a raven's nest on the headland. I climbed over the stone dam, jumping down to a place out of the wind, pleasantly warmed by the sun.

I was now hidden from the waiting heron by a screen of ash boughs cut and laid along the top of the bank. Shoots and twigs growing upright gave cover for my head as I peered under a horizontal grey bough. The heron was still standing in the farther field, among last year's thistle stalks and grass-clumps, its head held high and anxious. It was doubtful if it had the sense of continuity: that it would remember I had not reappeared.

I had been standing there for about a minute when rustlings and small thumpings became audible on the bank, with the squeaks of rats. I had forgotten the rats. Were they fighting over the frog brought into the tunnels when first I had sat by the pond?

I listened, keeping still; and peering over the dam, I saw a rat running along the side of the pond, followed by two other rats. They made straight for the omnibus—still in the attitude of breakdown—and through my glass I watched two rats pulling the frogs apart. The jockey, the green super-jockey, and the aspirant hung on to each other, kicking and croaking; but the rats, the zestful and murderous rats, braced their hind legs and bit and tugged, The aspirant was the first to go; he was dragged immediately along the path to the hole. Vainly the green super-jockey croaked for speed; he was nipped by a leg, but the strength of two tugging rats could not shift him. After a while, for a minute I should think, the rats ceased to pull each for himself; they appeared to organize themselves, and set about removing the omnibus as it stood. Each with a leg in its mouth, and with heads held high, they trotted along the bank, sharing the weight of muscled frogflesh.

Another rat ran to meet them, and yet another. There was a squeak and scuffle, and the newcomers ran on, plainly told to mind their own affairs. They ran to the water, where, putting their heads down, they swam under like small unskilful otters.

Squeaks inside the bank told me that the rats had entered with their booty, and I remained there, hoping to get a glimpse of them, for there were many rabbit holes in the bank. Noises of tugging and thumping came with more squeaks out of a low tunnel, and tiring of my position, I stood upright again to watch the swimming rats. Long thin legs and wide grey wings upheld and dropping blurred in the retina of my eye: the heron had flown back to the pond.

It folded its wings, while raising its head and looking round for movement that might mean danger. Knowing how keen was the sight of this shy bird, I tried not to blink an eyelid, for the section of my face under the laid ash-bough was silhouetted (from the heron's point of view) against the sky.

Suddenly the heron lowered its beak. I saw a rat swimming across the pond, its whiskered head exposed with something unwieldy before it. It was carring a frog. The heron's body, seeming so loose and thin within the shell of soft grey wings, their big flight quills tipped with black, seemed to stiffen and sharpen. It moved head and neck low and forward, an unobtrusive action against the background of its body. The rat could not have seen it, for it swam on steadily until it was within twenty inches of the heron's sharp beak, when the beak struck and the rat was lifted out of the water. It squealed and twisted; its feet ran on air; its tail whipped its body. The heron turned round to strike it on the bank, but its beak was wedged in the rat's skull. It lifted a long leg and tried to claw it with its toes, and the weight of the rat and the wind caused it to stagger.

Then the heron saw my eyes under the bough of the ash tree, and jumped into the air with fright. It flapped and tumbled; but before I had time to clamber over the bank, it had recovered, and was steady on the wing. In the air it clawed its beak again, and the rat fell with a splash into the water. When I reached the bank opposite the splash I saw a dead rat floating in the wavelets, with a jockey already riding on its shoulders, croaking defiance to another whose head, set with glazed and bulging eyes, was poked up alongside.

SWAGDAGGER CROSSES A FIELD

There is something in the nature of most men, arising on certain uneasy occasions, which has a basis so universal that everywhere it commands the sympathetic understanding of reasonable folk—an attitude of which the commonest vocal expression is 'Why do you want to interfere with me? I don't want to interfere with you! But if you're looking for trouble you'll damn'd well find it!' And as with men, so with animals who live the life, wild and free and pitiless, that men, more or less—chiefly less—have quit.

This attitude in the wild is liable to instant reverse; the trouble seeker of one moment may be the troubled of the next. The rights and wrongs—many of them as old as life itself—of Swagdagger happily crossing a field on a certain morning in early June cannot be discussed in this story, which is able only to hold an account of all the trouble which began when I looked over the western bank of my hilltop property in North Devon—a field I had recently bought.

Who had been leaving litter in my field? There the evidence was—a long strip of paper, blowing across the grass! I had seen no-one there a moment before, when I had been in the field.

The sooner a proper palisade gate replaced the ramshackle tangle of rotten bars and posts, the better! Also, I must see that the gap in the bank—made by bullocks, so the farmer had said—was filled with level thorn branches pegged down.

I vaulted over this formless ruin, meaning to pick up the paper; but when I got to where it had lain, it was gone. Had a magpie picked it up for a nest lining? But magpies always built with dark twigs, and put a top of thorns to cover the nest.

Three red lanes, metal'd with ironstone—one of them already bearing much motor traffic in summer—met at the south-western corner of the field, near the deciduous gate. Just above this gate was a small spinney of beech trees which I call Windwhistle Cross. The road divides the spinney, and leads on over the down to Ilfracombe. It was toward these trees that I had looked when I passed the gap in the bank. Now, I considered myself to be both shrewd and observant; yet it only occurred to me a few moments later that the long white strip, rippling as paper in wind, had been moving in a direction *contrary* to that in which the wind was blowing.

As I was soon to learn, the white object in the middle of the field was moving on a track it had run along many times before, a track belonging to itself. Indeed, it owned the entire field, with every other field it ran in. Its sense of ownership was similar to that of my own, but more elemental; its angry defiance of any intrusion was coupled with a raging desire to break with teeth the jugular vein of its enemy. Nearly everything was its enemy, and nearly everything ran from it; for it was Swagdagger the stoat. Swagdagger lived a life harder and more eventful than any other stoat in the West Country, for he had been born without colour, except for his eyes, which were pink, and the tip of his tail, which was black. Swagdagger's hairy coat, covering a long and sinuous body, was white as the snow which so seldom fell in the fields. Nearly everything saw Swagdagger as he ran prowling, low and swift and sniffing the air, over green pasture and brown ploughland, and through the thorns and brambles growing on the banks dividing the fields.

During the days that followed, I, keeping up wind, and focusing my Zeiss monocular, saw much of Swagdagger, as I called him. He was usually hurrying, but not always hunting. Many times a day he ran with eagerness across his fields into Windwhistle Cross, to play with the five stoats who lived under a wood stack at the foot of a beech tree. Such rough-and-tumble games they played together— Swagdagger, his mate, and their cubs.

One morning as he moved in the field a dark brown bird, with a wing span of more than four feet, wheeled in the sky a quarter of a mile away, and slanted down over the wind-sheared tree tops of the spinney. Swagdagger saw it coming, and ran faster. It was a buzzard hawk, whose wailing cry often came down from the sky. It fed on rabbits, moles, and snakes, which it dropped on from above and clutched in its yellow feet, piercing with black talons, and tearing with its hooked beak. The hawk was stronger and much heavier than the stoat, who saw its eyes and beak and hanging legs, under the line of outspread wings, grow larger and larger as it glided upon him. Swagdagger stopped, forepaws on ground, head and neck raised and pointing at the buzzard. He crouched until it lifted great wings to drop on him, and then he stood on his hind legs. The buzzard, who had meant to grip him across the back, saw a small white flattened circle, set with whiskers, that broke across with sharp clicking teeth.

The stoat stood like a lean mushroom stalk; the hawk seemed to bounce off its angry pointed nose. It flapped broad wings, to keep safely above the furious pale eyes. It flapped heavily over the stoat toward the spinney, but rippling white movement lured it back again. It turned and swept down on the stoat, spreading yellow toes for the attack. The white ripple stopped, becoming fixed and upright under the snatch of talons. Again the buzzard quailed before the snapping teeth, and, beating into the air, sent a wailing cry down the wind. *Whee-ee-i-oo!*

Another bird, black from bristled beak to toe, that was perching on the highest bough of an elderberry tree, stunted and lichen-crusted at the south-western point of the spinney, heard the cry, and started out of its reverie— for it was contemplating the old nest from which it had driven the last of its grown winglings that morning. Immediately it stretched its head higher. Every black feather tightened when it saw the buzzard. Its craw swelled, its tail dipped, its beak opened, and *Scarl! Scarl!* it called, harshly and rapidly.

Another carrion crow heard the call, and left the broken carcass it had been eating—rabbit in snare set by labourer—and flew toward the elderberry. The crows built their nest in one or other of the trees of Windwhistle Cross every year; they owned the spinney and the fields around it, and whenever they saw a winged or a four-legged intruder they drove it away from their property.

Krok! Krok!—*Hawk! Hawk!* said the first crow, flying up to meet her mate. Together they flew, silently, just above the green slope of the wind-sheared tree tops. They appeared suddenly over the spinney, seeing the field below. *Krok! Krok! Krok!* said the crow again, and flew faster toward the buzzard, meaning to peck out its feathers—a thing which the crows tried to do whenever they flew near a buzzard, not liking its face.

Before its beak had closed again, the male crow saw the stoat. Scarl had seen Swagdagger many times before. *Krarr! Krarr! Krarr!* cried Scarl and his mate together, turning across the wind, and slanting over the red lane and the bramble-grown bank.

Every day, antagonism increased between stoat and crow. Usually, Swagdagger was not far from Windwhistle Cross when the crows dived at him. He recognized the voice of Scarl, and ground his teeth. With open beak Scarl dived, but a yard from the ground the crow flattened his wings and with a jeering *Krarr!* passed over him. Scarl alighted two yards behind Swagdagger, while his mate flapped above and in front of him. The stoat stood up to meet the peck of the crow, and Scarl, hopping quickly over the grass from behind, nipped the black tip of his tail.

In this way they teased Swagdagger, while he grew more and more angry. Every time he attempted to run forward he was poked and jabbed from behind by one or another of the crows, and still he was not far from the bank whence he had started.

Meanwhile the buzzard was soaring higher, watching the shifting white streak. It was being stared at by a bird perched on a thorn growing out of the eastern bank of the field. This bird was the size of a crow, but more huddled-looking; and it had a whitey-grey face of bare skin. The buzzard saw it looking up, and wailed for its mate again. The grey-faced bird launched itself off the thorn, and with leisured beat of wings climbed into the air to look around. It was a sentinel rook, and the buzzard was wary of rooks, for often they mobbed him.

It flew under the hawk, and cried *Caa! Caa-r!* Hearing the summons, several rooks looked up from the earth where they were digging new potatoes. Buzzard never harmed, and potatoes were good. They went on digging again, knowing the old self-appointed sentinel rook to be at times over-officious.

Now Scarl the carrion crow saw the rook flying under the buzzard, and, I feel sure, began to *think*. First one eye was cocked at them, then the other—for a crow does not reason until he has taken a double squint. His beak lifted higher, his craw swelled, he dipped, and *Krok-krok-krok-krok!* he cried. The stoat bounded upon him, but the crow, still looking at the sky, hopped over his head, alighted behind him, and gave four more croaks. *Ca-ar!* answered the sentinel rook, leaving the buzzard, and flying over the field to find out why crow had called him. He saw, turned, and flew back quickly, in silence.

Usually rooks flew wide of crows, whom they distrusted, for crows had been known to chase the little red mousehawks, or kestrels, over their rookery in spring, and, in the general uproar that greeted the hawk, to sneak into the trees and suck rooks' eggs. But against Swagdagger every bird's beak and wing was raised. *Krok-krok-krok-krok!* cried the rook, wheeling over the edge of the potato patch, and calling them in a voice like a crow's. This time every rook flew up. The potato diggers (my potatoes) glided and swooped down to the grass as soon as they saw the white ripple. They filled the air with cawing and the sound of wings. They alighted to make around the stoat a rough excited circle, which broke wherever Swagdagger ran in his grinding rage.

Each rook appeared to be urging its neighbour to hop forward and dab him one on the head. Each rook was determined not to be the one to dab first. Their wide and simple eyes, filled with scared thoughts, looked from stoat to crow, from crow to one another. Scarl and his mate hopped about in the ring, feeling safe with so many beaks near them, and enjoying the game of peck and jump. And all the while they were playing the crows were watching their chance to peck out Swagdagger's eyes.

Sometimes nervous rooks would fly up with squawks of alarm, but the croaks of the bolder crows were reassuring, and they alighted in the circle again. Jackdaws passing over the spinney dropped among them, like flakes of burnt paper out of the blue sky, and croaked with deep voices, for they too belonged to the powerful family of *Corvidae*, sharing ownership of all the fields and woods. They poked their grey polls and hard azure eyes between the dishevelled shoulders of the rooks, and cursed Swagdagger, who in hot rage was giving off a most penetrating stench, which in itself was almost enough to keep them at a distance. Then came four magpies, sloping over the field, their wings flickering black and white as they made slow way against the wind. They scolded loudly when they saw Swagdagger. After them came a pair of missel thrushes, who flew down boldly, the smallest birds present, and screamed in the face of Swagdagger as he stood, with swishing tail, with bared teeth, with blazing eyes, in a green space enclosed by the black and shifting mass. Suddenly every bird looked up into the air, and remained motionless, as though frozen.

Three miles westward, on his pitch two thousand feet above the sea, Chakchek the Backbreaker, the peregrine falcon, had seen the commotion of wings in the field, and a white speck in the centre.

His family owned the air of the world; even the eagle shifted under his stoop. Across the sky on level pinions he had glided, cutting round into the wind above Windwhistle Cross. He saw upheld beaks and eyes watching him anxiously. Crows and a stoat! He turned, and swept away.

2

The sentinel rook, sire of many birds of the rookery in the village below, an old bird whose life was set in duty to others, watched the Backbreaker an eye-blink longer than the other rooks watched. He forgot Swagdagger as he stared at the pointed wings, which often he had heard hissing in the dreaded stoop. Then a whiteness flashed, and the old rook was on his back, his feathers were flying, his legs were kicking. He tried to screech a warning, but as his beak opened he shuddered; and Swagdagger, red on teeth and whiskers, ran at the next rook. The grass was flattened by the draught of beating wings.

Cra! cried Scarl, who had jumped a yard, but alighted again. *Cra!* as he hopped to the stricken rook, and pecked out his eyes.

As soon as the rooks and daws had flown up, Swagdagger started to run towards the spinney, carrying his head high. He had gone one third of the way along his track when the rooks, flying at him with open beaks, but swerving a safe distance off, checked him again. Other birds came to the field—tomtits and wagtails, sparrows, finches, and stonechats. They perched on the brambles of the banks, each one adding his tick or squall or stitter to the

general outcry. Some of them had lost mates or fledglings
when last they had seen the white horror.

Kron-n-n-n-n-n-k!

The sound, prolonged and deep, was audible through
the screeching and cawing. It came from above the spinney. Swagdagger stopped, sniffing the air. Only one thing
had such an acrid smell, and whenever he encountered it
Swagdagger got out of daylight into the nearest rabbit
hole.

The owner of the deep and penetrating voice had flown
inland when he had seen Chakchek the Backbreaker slip
off his pitch; for sometimes he robbed the falcon of what
he had struck down. The raven alighted on a branch at the
top of a tree, which bowed to his weight. Scarl the crow
saw him—he was perching on Scarl's own lookout
branch, which commanded nearly all the ground around
the spinney—but Scarl said nothing. For the newcomer
was Kronk, King of the Crows, the powerful and aged
owner of seven miles of coast—from Pencil Rock to the
Morte Stone, where the realm of his great-grandson, the
Gaping Raven, began—and of thousands of acres of forest,
heath, field, spinney, and down.

Kron-n-n-k!

The raven, looking blacker than any crow, he was so
big, jumped off the lookout branch, and climbed almost
vertically into the air. When about twenty feet above the
tree tops he rolled on one wing, dropped a yard, and rolled
level again. Then, his playful movement over, he pointed
his great black beak at the stoat, and glided down to kill
him.

But Swagdagger did not wait while Kronk was growing bigger in his downward glide. He turned, and galloped
back along the track he had started to follow more than ten
minutes before. *Whee-oo!* cried the buzzard from the sky,
soaring on still, cleaver-shaped wings, as he watched
Swagdagger fleeing before more than fifty clamorous
birds, almost to be overtaken by the fast raven.

Swagdagger rippled up the bank, and got among the top cover. The withered sword grasses, and tough strings of bindweed tying brambles and briars, and dry thorn branches laid lengthways across old bullock-broken gaps, moved and rustled as he drew his lean body under them. Crows and rooks followed him, flapping to where patches of white showed in the long net of grasses, below stalks of tansy, dock, and hogweed. Three times he was pecked as he travelled along the southern bank, but he reached the corner safely, and turned up the western bank towards Windwhistle Spinney.

He pushed his sharp way among the brambles and grasses to the break made by the feet of bullocks scrambling over into the sunken lane below—where first I had seen the white paper, as I had thought of it. The gap of earth and stone was bare for two yards. On a stone bedded in the dry earth stood the great raven.

Now stoats—and their smaller relations, the weasels—possess strength and determination which last in fullness unto the moment of death; and the mind of Swagdagger was set upon getting to Windwhistle Cross. His small flat head pushed out of the grasses, moved up and down, swung sideways, while the nostrils worked nervously at all the hostile scents. The quick movements wove a hole in the grasses, which set around the thin neck like a collar. The gaze of the eyes wandered, then it rested on Kronk, standing a yard away.

Raven and stoat remained still, brown and pink eyes fixed in the same stare. All the lithe furious power of Swagdagger blazed in his eyes, for he dared not run forward. His tail swished the grasses behind him; fumes of anger drove the rooks into the upper air. And then, suddenly, at a new short *Kra!* from Scarl the crow, the clamour ceased, and the air above Swagdagger's head emptied of wings. Raven, crows, rooks, daws, pies, thrushes, finches, tits, all flew away silently, big birds over the field, little birds along the hedge, leaving Swagdagger alone.

The stoat stepped through his grassy collar, smelled only furze bloom and foxglove in the air, saw the birds flying away, and forgot them. Without hesitation he ran down the bank and across the grass to his track; for he had never entered Windwhistle Spinney any other way.

He was near the northern bank when the noise of wings made him stop and throw up his head. The buzzard which had been sitting on the bank by the far corner, watching in curiosity the behaviour of the birds, had been alarmed when they had suddenly flown away; but not having heard what they had seen in the sunken lane beyond, and being fearful of taking the air when raven and crow were about, it had continued to sit there. The white moving lure of Swagdagger was too strong for its caution; it forgot the general alarm, and flew over to the stoat.

On broad brown wings it sank upon Swagdagger, flapping to check its glide and stiffening its legs for the clutch. Swagdagger stood up to meet it with his teeth, but, as the buzzard was about to strike, it looked away, apparently startled by my face, set with the grey Zeiss glass.

The buzzard's wings beat violently in alarm; and instantly they beat wildly, for Swagdagger's teeth had pierced one of its legs above the knee. It rose up above the level of the bank, and tumbled sideways, the weight of the stoat struggling and twisting under it.

The buzzard unclenched its feet to be free, but they were clutched on nothing. It dived and tumbled, but could not shake off the jerking weight on its leg. It dropped towards the field again, meaning to stand on the stoat and rip it up with its hooked beak, as it had ripped up many rats and rabbits, but the shout of a man made it fly up into the air.

Many feathers floated away in the wind over the spinney, as the hawk swooped and tumbled and recovered. The rooks, back at their potato digging (my potatoes), looked up at the struggle. Some flew around the buzzard as it zigzagged overhead, and added their cawing to the wailing whistle of the hawk. Swagdagger held to the leg with his teeth and the long claws of his forepaws, and whenever the buzzard's beak came forward to cut open his head he loosened his bite and snapped at the throat. Sometimes his tail was over his head, as he swung to the turns and somersaults of his enemy.

The flight took them away over the adjacent grazing field. I hastened to the gate, and saw that the wings of the buzzard appeared to be flapping more heavily, and its tumblings were slower. Two claws of its right uninjured foot had pierced the loose skin of Swagdagger's neck, and were clenched tightly. It flew as before, in and out of the cawing rooks, until its bitten leg began to give it pain, it twirled and wailed towards the ground.

A final frenzied tumble in the air flung Swagdagger's head near its own, and the buzzard's beak opened to break his skull; but Swagdagger was quicker, and his teeth, like two rows of bone thorns, sank into the feathers of the buzzard's throat. The feathers sailed away, and he snapped again, but his teeth did not click. Hanging there, he steadily changed colour, his head and back and dripping tail, from white to dark red, while both predators sank down to the earth. There the hawk began to strike with its feet and buffet with its wings while snapping its beak; but Swagdagger held on, his eyes closed as he drew warm strength from his enemy.

The dying hawk flapped upon the ground, Swagdagger rippled away, leaving a trail of small feathers sticking to the grasses. The idea of getting to his mate was still, apparently, firmly fixed in his mind. He galloped gleefully, licking his jaws as he thought of the game he would play with his cubs.

He reached my field, and ran along his track. Halfway across he stopped, his nose working at the air that came in swirls from the bank. There was the smell of fresh-turned earth, blown with a strange and puzzling taint. He left his track, making a loop to avoid the unseen danger; for everything strange was dangerous to Swagdagger. Ten yards off the north bank he seemed to freeze, for his nostrils had dipped into a stream of strong, familiar scent—my own.

I had heard of stoats having a strange power to scare men, and decided to find out what this one would do, after his recent exertions. So I started after him, shouting "Hi!" when Swagdagger ran up the bank. When I got to the place where Swagdagger had climbed, I saw nothing there.

Picking up a stick (just in case) I hurried round the outside corner of the lane. I was in time to see a tail, tipped with black, disappear over the low bank at the edge of the spinney. I scrambled through the brambles, holding out an arm to ward off low branches from knocking my face. Grasping the stick firmly, and with head held tense, I walked warily through the beech trees, peering left and right.

I came to a woodpile, and had a glimpse of a smaller animal, with white patches on its light brown body, before it disappeared. Exhilarated by excitement, I crept forward, and waited for it to run out again. I could almost touch it with my stick. Of course I didn't want to kill it, merely to see what it would do. I saw another peep out, and then another.

I began to pull at a branch of the top of the pile. I felt strong as I levered it up, and with a vigorous turning movement threw it down. Lovely white skins: they must be ermines! I saw myself in the midst of wondering villagers, but swiftly thought, *No, keep it quiet!* as I levered another heavy bough off the top of the pile. I was enjoying myself immensely.

I had thrown down four boughs when Swagdagger ran out of the pile. Swagdagger was in a rage. He had been pestered and thwarted nearly all the morning, his play was interrupted (four cubs rolling him over and biting him with their milk teeth) and now his mate and cubs were threatened. He stood still, uttering whiny, champing noises—for a translation of which into colloquial English see the first paragraph of this story. When I moved forward with uplifted stick, Swagdagger also moved forward. His harsh chakkering cry rattled in the spinney. He continued to approach me—fourteen inches of warning and aggression—and I heard myself saying, "*Grrr!* Get out of it, you beast!" as I held up the stick.

Hak! Hak! Hak! Hak! Hak! Hak!

I have been accused by 'scientific' chaps of anthropomorphism in my writing about animals; but I have always believed that birds and animals are near in instincts and feelings to men and women, being of the original flesh and spirit; what I hadn't realized was that Swagdagger's forefathers had run in Windwhistle Cross since the beech spinney had been planted nearly a century ago by a Devon landowner with an eye to adding beauty to the skyline. I was a little surprised, therefore, when Swagdagger ran forward and started to climb up my trousers. I yelled when the sharp claws pricked my knee, and struck at the animal with my hand; but so quick was Swagdagger, and so sure his eye, that he bit through the tip of a finger before a blow knocked him off.

I turned to leave the spinney. I heard myself shouting for help when I saw other little animals running out of the woodpile. I blundered through the low branches to the bank, brambles clawing my clothes, and filling me with fear. I stopped in the lane, and to my horror saw that I was being followed. *Hak! Hak! Hak! Hak! Hak! Hak!*

Wheeling high over Windwhistle Cross, above the rooks and crows, Kronk the raven must have seen me legging it down the lane, now oddly stimulated by *fear*.

I was pulling my Zeiss glass out of its case when the skewbald pack of Swagdagger ran round the corner.

Hak! Chakker! Hak!

I ran to the middle of my field, then turned, and stared at the pack. I felt a dreadful desire to remain standing still.

High in the air the raven, who also must have felt the fascination of being approached by a pack of hunting

stoats, watched me standing still until the white threads
were almost to me. Only then did I make for the lower
bank. I scrambled up, and stood among the brambles,
until the damned white threads reached the bank. I jumped
down with head turned to see if they were following.

Hak! Hak! Chakker-hak!

Wheeling on firm wings, the raven watched me haring
across the next field, and the plunging canter of bullocks
down wind when they got the musky scent of stoat. He
watched me across another field, and so to the road.

I ran on, slower and slower, groaning that if I only got
out of this, I would give up smoking. I was chased almost
to the cottage at the bottom of the hill, where a cattle dog,
which had been lying in the roadway, got up and loped
forward to see what the trouble was; and made off at full
speed when it smelled and saw.

Swagdagger appeared to forget all about me; he went
under a gate into another field, where was one of his
playgrounds, a quarry, from which ironstone had been
blasted for the widening of the motor road, and which the
brambles were always trying to reclaim. Here I fancy they
played awhile, and hunted rabbits, and washed themselves
after their meal, imitating Swagdagger, who was busy with
his tongue on ribs and back and tail. When they had played
again, the white leader led the way back to Windwhistle
and crossed my field for what was probably the first time
with that season's jolly cubs.

We grew to respect each other; to live and let live. I saw
the old predator sometimes; but kept my distance!

THE YELLOW BOOTS

Unlike many Hunts, the Inclefell Harriers—who also
hunted fox—held a meet on the day before their annual
Hunt Ball, and not the day after. The meet on the morning
of the last Hunt Ball will be remembered long. The
mounted followers and those on foot waited till midday,
but no pack was led to the crossroads. The meet had been
advertised in the local papers to be held at eleven o'clock.
At a quarter to twelve about one-third of the field, including every farmer, had gone homewards. A few minutes
after noon Jim Huggins rode up. He was the huntsman, an
old and fog-seasoned man. In his high voice he said that he
had been sent to say, with the Master's compliments, that
the meet was cancelled. That was all. In answer to questions, he made but one reply—"I don't know, s'm". It was
his habit to address both ladies and gentlemen as "s'm".
He never said "sir" or "ma'am".

"But what's happened, Jim? Anything the matter with
hounds?"

He sat upright and still on his stocky bay cob.

"I don't know, s'm."

"But how exraordinary! Are they sick?"

A week ago they had been fed on donkey flesh, and had
fought in the kennels, all the way to the meet, and even
when drawing covert. The unusual diet had been the cause
of many jokes.

"I don't know, s'm."

"Is General Inclefell all right?"

They walked their hunters nearer to him. They were
made curious by his rigid reticence.

"I don't know, s'm."

He shifted slightly on his right thigh the angle of his
whip.

"You don't know! Haven't you seen the Master this morning, Jim?"

The kennels, and the huntsman's cottage, were in a wood two hundred yards behind the Manor.

"Not this morning, s'm. Second footman came with the General's message, s'm."

"Have you seen Miss Mollie?"

She was the honorary whipper-in to her father's hounds.

"Not this morning, s'm."

Jim in his green cap and green coat sat on his bay cob, looking straight ahead, avoiding every eye. He was like a gnarled and mossy limb of one of the dwarf oaks of Wistman's Wood—trees rooted on Dartmoor, thick as they are tall, and said to be ancient before Domesday.

The voice of a boy said timidly:

"Plaize, zur, us didden hear no dogs zinging this morning."

"Hold your rattle, young tacker!" commanded Jim Huggins in the sharp, hound-rating voice he had not used since whiphood days. Only his jaw moved; the mist of breath vanished in the cold air. He looked at his horse's ears. People exchanged glances. The tacker was abashed.

He lived near the kennels, whence had come no singing of hounds that morning.

"Good day, s'm," said Jim, raising his cap, laying the near rein on the horse's neck and pressing its off flank with his boot. The cob turned with smart obedience and trotted home. The word "extraordinary" was ejaculated by nearly everyone present in the saddle.

That night, while people were arriving at the Bedford Hotel in Tavistock for the Hunt Ball, the secretary— 'Pops' Russell, who often said that life would be a bore without hunting, billiards, and Bass's beer—was surrounded by many black- and pink- and green-coated friends, to whom he told the astounding news that neither

Bimbo nor Moll was coming that evening.

"But, Pops, old man, what's up with Bimbo? What's all this mystery about?"

Bimbo was the name by which the Master was known to his friends.

"Asked me to tell you he was awfully sorry, but he isn't feeling very fit."

"And Moll?"

"Same, 'parently."

Everyone was discussing the peculiar happening. Somehow by supper time it was known that the entire pack had been destroyed. It was incomprehensible, for the Master was known everywhere for his fatherly tenderness to the hounds. However, the dance went merrily on. The band was voted a good one.

At two o'clock in the morning 'Pops' Russell and three of his pals were drinking in the bar. The middle-aged secretary was drinking his thirteenth bottle of Bass.

"What's the mystery, Pops?" asked 'Naps' Sprey-combe, M.F.H. in another country.

"Rioted," replied Captain Russell, staring at the lethargic bubbles rising to the flattened froth half-way down his glass. He was an honest man who disliked sub-terfuge, but he had to lie. "I suppose it's bound to get known, anyhow. Won't do hunting any good."

With a sudden movement he emptied his glass. "Don't tell anyone I told you. Rioted after sheep. Bimbo's poisoned 'em, every dog and every little bitch. Cyanide of potassium."

"Strewth!" drawled Spreycombe. "What about your committee? And subscribers?"

"That's the very devil of it," muttered the secretary. "I shall have the dirty work of explaining to subscribers. Bimbo's got enemies and they're not his own hounds—or weren't, I should say. There'll be the very devil if anyone gets nasty."

"Was it that run on Monday, when they got lost in the

mist?" inquired a young man wearing the uniform of the
Lamerton Hunt.

Captain Russell nodded.

"Put up hare, changed to a screaming scent up by Links
Tor—must have been fox, I think—disappeared into the
mist. Jim couldn't find'm. Stragglers began to come into
kennels about eight hours later. Moll heard'm in Tavy
Cleave, and saw'm eating sheep. Everyone of'm eating.
Once get the flavour of hot mutton, and it's all up with
your chance of catching fox or hare. Myself I believe it was
that dem donkey flesh."

Next day the *West Country Morning News* published a
statement, displayed prominently, that Major-General
T. F. M. Inclefell, C.M.G., D.S.O., the Master of the
Inclefell Harriers, had destroyed the entire pack for sheep
worrying. It was followed, in the issues of succeeding
days, by an extended correspondence. General Inclefell
was accused of acting hastily; he was held blameworthy for
the faulty and irregular feeding of hounds in kennels. The
incident was amplified into a general attack upon fox- and
hare- and stag-hunting. A letter signed W. H. Starcross,
Lt.-Col., R.E., complained of the expense the writer 'had
undergone in bringing hunters to the district and the en-
forced dismissal of his two temporary grooms in the worst
part of the winter consequent upon the folly of General
Inclefell shown by the needless and callous annihilation of
the innocent hounds with the guilty'. The secretary replied, stating that he had searched the Army List, and his
Subscribers' List, and had been unable to find the name of
W. H. Starcross in either.

This surprised everyone, except the writer of the letter,
an eighteen-year-old youth named Cocks, a mechanic to
an unqualified dentist, whose hunting experiences were
confined to (1) stalking lovers in the summer evening
fields, and (2) stamping mice to death during the threshing
of a corn-rick in his uncle's farmyard.

There were letters from *Not a Nut-Eater*, who wrote

about the "Appalling danger of rabies *via* the butcher's shop"; from *Dog-Lover*, who wrote "on behalf of poor little dogs who cannot defend themselves"; from *Only a Schoolgirl*—"We of the Upper Fifth have had a debate, and we have decided to let it be known that it was a jolly rotten thing to kill hounds. *Two blacks never yet made a white*, was our unanimous conclusion"; and from indignant butchers in Plymouth, answering the allegations of *Not a Nut-Eater*. And various others. Some funny, some silly; but all based upon ignorance.

Every letter was read in the West Country Club with great interest and often amusement, except by the uneasy Captain Russell, the secretary of the packless Hunt. His ruddy face appeared every day for its morning Basses, which were drunken, as usual, under the stuffed badger in the case above the fireplace. Often he declared that he wasn't interested in what was said, and as often he spent the morning morosely interested in what was said. He knew the main facts about the run in moorland fog, as told by a pale Molly Inclefell to her father in the evening of the disastrous Monday; and they were quite different from the explanation given at the Extraordinary General Meeting a few days later.

It was remarked that the Master had looked "positively uneasy, when Valentine Potstacker got up on his hind legs" and demanded the name of the farmer to whom compensation would be paid for the loss of sheep by worrying. The Master said that he would personally investigate and settle all claims. Major Potstacker, a lawyer speaking for a clique of subscribers, repeated that he would very much like the meeting to know the name of the farmer who had lost sheep by worrying. The Master replied in a voice weary but courteous that the Scotch sheep on the moors roamed at large; that some time must elapse before any loss could be discovered. Major Potstacker, following his line, suggested that all claims that were to be made had been notified already.

The Secretary then got up and said that surely everybody except the only non-subscriber present had been able to grasp what the Master had just told the meeting: that the committee would be called upon to examine no claims whatsoever, in respect of sheep worried by the pack. And further, he himself, as secretary, would announce that the Master, whom he understood was about to offer his resignation to the committee (which, in passing, he would say, he hoped would not be accepted). To that he would add that the Master had guaranteed the cost of a new pack. He sat down, feeling hot.

Major Potstacker thereupon said, gently, that he was representing some of the subscribers, and that on their behalf he would like to suggest that the price of new hounds would be the only expense to be borne by the Master and that he would further suggest that the Master might possibly have had another reason than the one given for the slaughtering of the hounds . . . Voices said, "Oh, shut up"; "Put a curb in his mouth someone"; and "Sit down, sit down".

Captain Russell jumped on his feet and said, "Mean to say I'm a liar?" Major Potstacker said, "Certainly not, Mr Secretary. I am seeking information. Now, I see many farmers present, men who call a spade a spade . . .' (A quiet voice: "Us calls'n shovels, maister," and laughter.) . . . "Well, shovels. Now farmers are exact in what they say; they insist on a shovel being called a shovel." And when loud laughter of only the farmers had ceased, Major Potstacker said distinctly, "Who among you lost sheep by worrying last Monday?" He looked round. "No one claims a loss! Well then. Who among you has counted your sheep?" Many gave an immediate "Aiy, aiy!" At this point he was called to order, and told curtly to address his questions to the chair. "Dem swine," Captain Russell was heard to mutter.

Major Potstacker knew that no sheep had been killed.

He had been making inquiries; but he had learned only negative information. And after the meeting, although he tried to pump Jim Huggins, he got nothing from him. "Warn't ee to the meeting, s'm?" Jim murmured plainly. "Aw, ee missed a rare lot o' rattling; but I be dalled if I knaws what 'twas all about." Yet even Jim, close and firm as a Wistman oak, didn't know everything.

2

The cracked tenor bell of the church had ceased its frang-ing hum when a man crawled furtively through the garderobe hole at the base of the wall of Lydford Castle. The four walls of this Norman ruin were open to the stars; the ivy pushing its roots into the yellow mortar between the hewn granite blocks and inner rubble shook with the exploring winds. The crumbling hollow square stood upon a motte, or raised mound of earth. For centuries it had been used as a stannary prison, but now its dungeon was fallen in; brambles grew where men had lain in chains. Owls and jackdaws cried around the walls by night and by day.

In the north-eastern wall of the keep was a mural chamber, built for hiding in an age of violence; it was dilapidated, the home of grasses and nettles. Stalks and blades were broken and bent; some blades were raising themselves, for the man who had been hiding in the wall all that Sunday, shivering and sometimes groaning, had just climbed along the ledge and jumped down. He was peering through the garderobe hole.

Once he had had a name; he still bore the name, but it was never spoken on any lips except his own. To have heard other men speaking the names bestowed upon him with pride and tenderness at his christening would have been to him warning of a calamity more terrible to antici-

pate than death. For he was one of the most wretched of
breathing things, a convict escaped from Princetown.

The number of his cell had been 76. He was known to
the warders as Seventy-Six—the warders to whom it was
forbidden to speak, unless he were asked a question. He
was Seventy-Six, a corrupted animal that for years had
quarried stone for other men's buildings, dug turf for
other men's fires, sewn bags for other men's letters; had
his hair cropped, his chin shaved, worn khaki clothes
marked with the possessive broad-arrow of His Majesty's
Government. An animal, not wild and pure, but with rot
in its mind, that had done with life, but with which life had
not yet done. He was godless.

The castle ruin was remembered from a happy visit
from Plymouth, just before the Great War, when he had
been on his honeymoon. From August 1914—when he
had jacked up his job and stood for hours before a recruit-
ing office, hoping with his pals to be sent off to fight before
the fun was ended—until his escape the day before, he had
had practically no sense of time. He had exchanged one
number of military servitude for another of penal
servitude with only one period of tentative freedom—
when he had murdered a man and a woman. Now he had
another interval of freedom. The day before, Seventy-Six,
who was serving a commuted death sentence, had
dropped, from the scaffolding where he had been working, a
block of stone on a warder's head, and escaped by running
through the fog. He had scooped in his hands the icy
waters of the moor, drinking on his knees. He had eaten
grass. Repeatedly he had touched the hem of his jacket,
fearful lest he might have lost his only companion.

Seventy-Six crept through the hole and listened. A row
of larches grew between the castle and the church. The fog
was gone, and moisture dripped from the branches. Or-
gan music came with a dim light through the windows of
the holy building. People were singing the evening
psalms. Seventy-Six sneered mentally.

After listening he slunk down the slope of the motte to the larches, jumped softly down a bank, and walked to a gate. Once again he listened, but hearing no footfalls climbed the gate and crossed the road. He entered the rectory garden, startling from a laurel bush a bird that flew away with shrill squealing cries of alarm. Seventy-Six cursed and touched his jacket again. Reassured by the contact of his index fingertip with the head of what he sought, he crept towards the house, stooping, with silent steps on the grass border of the main path.

A cautious inspection of the lightless building told him that all the lower windows were secured. He felt along one pane, wondering if he dare risk the noise of putting his elbow through it. While he was hesitating, he heard above the thudding of his heart the voices of men in the village street. He hurried away, going down a steep slope among spruce and larch trees where it was very dark, but safe. The river roared below in the gorge. He turned to the left, and walked on, often blundering into ants'-nests as tall as himself, and mossy-wet trunks of trees. He bruised his head, and a sudden mood of happiness came upon him.

The wood was thinner by a viaduct with arches that spanned the gorge. A thought came to him that it would be easy to climb the embankment and lay his head on the rail and end it all. But while he waited a train thundered above him. Sparks rained into the dark gorge. He was still free; but so hungry. Seventy-Six choked back a desire to cry, and walked on. The path was rough with shillets, and led down to a cottage before which were scattered bits of paper and empty tins. Washed underwear, some of it ragged, was thrown on a hedge in front. He scrounged two shirts and a pair of trousers hanging with the lining inside-out. He chucked one shirt back on the hedge, thinking that the bloke as owned it was a poor man.

An abandoned water-mill stood near a footbridge, with broken roof and walls, and he was about to explore when he heard a man's voice above the rushing sounds of the

river. Thinking that the owner of the clothes had discovered the loss, Seventy-Six crossed by the footbridge.
He had stepped down to the path on the other side when he
saw the glow of a cigarette in the darkness above him.
Someone was coming down the path through the wood.
He crouched on the earth, hiding his face, and felt about
for a stone or stick. The voice spoke again, high and eager,
and of the quality that Seventy-Six had often laughed at
when coming from the lips of music-hall comedians before the war. The red point came near, and now a girl was
speaking. Seventy-Six listened to the first feminine voice
he had heard since his trial at the Old Bailey.

"What fun, I say! But you know, we mustn't ever let
daddy know we did it."

"Rather not! I feel rather a rotter to have done it, really,
without his knowing. Of course, he doesn't hunt, but after
all I'm his guest. He's on the committee, too."

They stopped by the bridge.

"Shall we do it, Bid? Or shall we go up to the village and
make a present of it to old Atters? It's damned heavy to
carry."

"Oh, let's do it! Daddy will laugh when he hears,"
persuaded the girl. "He doesn't like Captain Russell for
killing all the badgers, but he didn't like to say anything, as
the farmer wanted them killed."

"The farmer was probably thinking of the free drinks
next month at the Badger Club supper," said the young
man scornfully. "And he probably believes they do harm,
as Russell says they do, the fat liar! The other day I heard
him telling someone in the West Country Club that he had
'dug out a hundred and thirty pounds of badger flesh from
one holt!' His very words. Whereas two labourers did the
digging, three terriers got bitten, one a broken jaw, and all
the work he did was sometimes to kneel at the hole,
thrusting down an ear to hear what was happening, and
then to tootle-too on a copper horn with what little beery
breath he possessed after his athletic feat of kneeling. Pah!

And, of course, he stabbed the poor brocks when someone had banged them on the nose with a shovel."

"Pah!" said the young girl delightedly. "He calls that *sport!*" The man's eager voice spoke as they were moving away. "You know, Bid, it will be a great scene when hounds leave the hare's line and crash off down to the marsh! And when Russell and the rest of them arrive at the holt—and find hounds at dinner!"

The conversation was meaningless for Seventy-Six, except the word dinner. He allowed them to get a safe distance ahead of him before following along a footpath under trees beside the river. He climbed a wooden fence, dropped down to a single plank over a ditch, and walked away from the river and up a path which lay on the rock, past a waterfall that thundered white in the darkness, and on to grass again.

Half an hour later, he was trying to find what they had been hiding on the side of a hillock above the marshy ground by the river. The word dinner had so filled his mind while he had been staring in the direction of the voices, that he was convinced they had been hiding food. Reasons for the concealment of food did not occur to him. He stopped among the furze and bracken, to get the dinner that was waiting for him if only he could find the right place. His forehead knocked a thorny branch, and he was rubbing the pain away when he fell into a hole, where immediately he smelled a strong smell. Wondering if it led to a cave where he might hide by day, he felt with his hands. Chopped roots stuck out of its sides and roof. It led about six feet into the gravelly earth. At its end the tunnel narrowed, and was blocked by something soft. He pulled out a heavy bundle and unwrapped the cloth round it, to feel a cold smooth object, with a rough covering. It was a pie.

Seventy-Six pushed his thumb through the crust, and tasted. He tore off the pastry, and pulled out a handful of meat. He crammed it into his mouth, swallowing without chewing, gulping with dry wheezings in his throat. He muttered and thought phrases like "Gorblime, mate, you're in luck," and "Stuff to give'm!" The food gave him sharp pains, and he went to the river to drink. When he returned, he ate less quickly. It was a steak and kidney pie, flavoured with onions and hard-boiled eggs. The gravy was rich, tasty with salt and pepper. The dish was big, holding enough for a dozen men.

When he had eaten his fill he again felt about the place. It ended in a tunnel too small for him to crawl into. He found a pair of light walking boots, with rubber pads fixed on the soles. With them were the skin of an animal, stuffed with straw, a coat, and a bowler hat. The smell he had noticed when he found the hole was thick on the skin. It dimly recalled the pain of caned hands in boyhood.

Some hours later, wandering on the lower heather slope of the moor, he found a hiding place under an oblong slab of granite. It was sealed on all sides save one, by which he entered. Low-growing furze and heather and whortle-berry formed a springy door. He crawled out again, and tore, with difficulty, handfuls of heather from the sodden ground, while a herd of small wild grazing cattle stared and sniffed near him. A wan white moon gleamed above low clouds moving over from the south-west. Seventy-Six made his bed, and placed in a far corner the dish with its life-making food. He wore the khaki, arrow-marked clothes no longer. At first he had hidden them in the pillaged badger-holt, but cunning had made him pull out the bundle, and, going back the way he had come, drop it, boots and all, in a waterfall of the gorge under the viaduct. But before discarding his prison clothes, he had withdrawn something from his jacket and placed it in the hem of the new coat.

To Seventy-Six, warm and happy, came the old thoughts he had had just before his marriage, when one Sunday night he had listened idly, his girl on his arm, to a street preacher, and believed what he had heard. He recalled another preacher before whom the battalion had been marched, and formed into a hollow square, and ordered to lie down, while the chaplain stood up and preached. The old sweats 'ad said afterwards that they were for it again, because the padre 'ad talked about Gawd being on their side, which 'e always did just before a push.

The words were realized now by Seventy-Six for the first time since that September church parade before Loos in 1915. Gawd saved sinners! Gawd had arranged for the pie to be hid there! He sat on the granite slab, and said "Gorblime!" which was the vocal accompaniment of his poor darkened spirit's aspiration. He did not really pray to be blinded.

A rising wind stirred the heather, and curlew cries were blown across the sky. Seventy-Six thought, Gawd, please go hon 'elping me. Then he drew out from the hem of his coat the thing he cared for more than anything on the earth, and played with it. It had been with him through his trial. He tossed it a few inches into the air, and caught it lightly between finger and thumb. He had played like this in his cell for hours, often watched by warders. It had shared his hopes for a better life—for Seventy-Six was still young enough to hope for a happier future. So acquainted was he with the ways of his companion that Seventy-Six could jerk it up and catch it again in the dark. He caught it by his front teeth and, biting on to its head, nicked it with a finger-nail. It made the least musical note, which was a loved voice, comforting him. It fell, and he trembled; his throat was dry until he found it. How glad he was when it prickled his finger, and he picked it up and put it in its place. It was an ordinary pin, made of brass, the bright plating of which had long since worn off.

Seventy-Six crawled into the refuge and fell into a deep sleep before he had tucked in his legs. All night the rain was driven slantingly upon his boots. An old dog-fox trotted down to where he lay, made curious by the strange scent carried upwind to Links Tor where it had been seeking beetles. Three stoats visited the boots during the

night; and when the rain ceased at daylight a pair of ravens,
flying to the moor from their rocky fastness in the gorge,
dipped from a height of two hundred yards to inspect the
yellow things in the heather. After much flapping of wings
and dipping of beaks over the granite slab, one dared to
alight. With sidling walk and glances of little eyes, and
uneasy hops into the air, it made a swift lunge with its
beak, ripping a toe-cap. A grunt from under the stone, and
the ravens departed, fearing a trap. They were puzzled as
the fox and stoats had been at the unfamiliar taint in the air.

3

A few hours later the Inclefell Harriers met at the Dartmoor Inn. A small field was present, about two dozen in
the saddle, including farmers. Miss Mollie Inclefell stood
talking to Jim Huggins the huntsman. She was a slight fair
girl, wearing black coat and breeches. Six motorcars had
brought people. The Squire was there, on foot with his
sons and daughters. With them was a young man who hid
a nervous restlessness under an assumed lack of interest in
the meet.

When the huntsman took hounds to a certain slope of
bracken where a hare was usually to be found, the
youngest daughter of the Squire set off with her companion, at a tangent from the curve made by the mounted
and foot followers. When over the brow of the slope they
started to run. Unseen, they crossed the river Lyd by
leaping on boulders. Quickly they climbed up the other
slope. The two friends were making for high ground
whence the old badger holt might be seen. For a quarter of
a mile they climbed in sunlight, and then they sat down on
an oblong block of granite embedded in heather.

They had been sitting down less than a minute when
hounds far away and below gave tongue. A hare had been

started from its form. The high voice of Jim Huggins sang
faintly in the wind. They watched the hare making a
right-handed turn towards the field of flat-poll cabbages
behind the Dartmoor Inn. The hare sped away from the
leading hounds. They watched it crossing the place where,
the previous afternoon, the young man had taken off his
brogues and pulled from a haversack a pair of yellow boots
. . . suddenly hounds checked, they clamoured, they
pushed their muzzles together so that they looked like a
great fungus suddenly grown on the moor, only to break
up into fragments that streamed along a new line. They
over-ran the place where the hare had branched, and raced
along the crest of the hill above the stream. The extended
field cantered behind.

When the young man turned to speak to the girl standing a few yards away, he was startled by her white cheeks.
She was staring at something near. Following her gaze, he
saw the pair of boots which he had imagined to be with
other things in the badger holt. The boots were covering
the sockless feet of a hidden man.

The girl whispered, "Oh, it may be the escaped
convict!"

The young man stared at the boots again, and said,
"Oh, my God!" Then he leapt through the heather and
clutched one of the heels. His hand was kicked away.

"Come out, I say," he said quickly. "There isn't a
moment to be lost."

"Oo are yer?" snarled a voice.

"On my honour I won't hurt you," cried the other,
certain that the man was the escaped convict. "You are
wearing the boots I hid in the badger holt. It was ment for a
joke. I really should advise you to clear off as soon as
possible."

He was deeply alarmed, and had tried to talk in an
ordinary voice to reassure his companion. She was a nervous and imaginative girl, but recently recovered from
scarlet fever.

"Why can't a bloke 'ave a bit of a kip if 'e wants to?" threatened the voice. And then, "If yer tries any monkey tricks, I'll bash yer, straight I will!"

"Please come away, please," implored the trembling girl, looking at her companion.

The baying of the pack grew fainter as hounds sank the hill to the holt two miles away. After more persuasion, the man came out, clutching a piece of granite in his left hand. He wore a pair of labourer's trousers with the lining on the outside, a grey shirt, a Lovat tweed jacket, and a grey bowler hat. The wan blue eyes of his ruined face looked about him with such an ailing wildness in them that the young man felt he had to deal with a madman.

"Don't be alarmed, I say," he said, aghast and smiling. "Look here, you ought really to clear off as quickly as possible. In about ten minute or less hounds may be running your line. I laid a drag yesterday with those boots you've got on now. Wherever you've been walking they may follow. Now if you'll only run to Links Tor over there on the skyline, you'll find a narrow crack in the granite, up which you can climb to the top. It's hard to get up the Chimney, but once there you'll be safe until they can whip hounds off. Look here, I'll follow you and give you a pound for the trouble you've had through my damned foolishness. And I'll give you my word I won't breathe a word to anyone that I've seen you. After all, I haven't the least idea who you are, and it's none of my business—I mean, not my affair who you are. Now go, as quick as you can."

Seventy-Six, having been born and bred in a Bermondsey slum, had never seen a live hound in his life. He looked at the summit of Links Tor.

"Climb up on the skyline to be sniped at, eh? Not a hope! See any green in my eye?"

The young man said earnestly. "Well, look here, change boots. I've got you in this mess, and I can run. But . . . all right, Bid, don't worry. But it wouldn't be any good, unless you hide that jacket! Clear off, there's a good fellow. Oh, my God, do hurry. Look, they're running to the badger holt."

The girl never forgot the look in the convict's eyes. She was unable to cry, she was fixed as though in a nightmare. The face became set in her mind, as a symbol, not of human spoliation and despair, but of cruelty and evil. She knew nothing of war. She heard him mutter something as he flung the granite lump at the face of her companion, who groaned and dropped into the heather. She could not breathe. She heard hounds in the distance, and thought, Come soon, come soon. She watched the blood beginning to run from the purple mark on his forehead. She was dizzy and sick, and vaguely realized that the man was ramming her father's old otter-hunting hat on his head as he ran. The hillside seemed to slide up the sky.

4

Long before he reached the tor, Seventy-Six had to use his hands to aid him. After splashing and slipping through soggy ground he came to a clitter of rocks overgrown with turf and mosses. A holly had its roots in a granite crevice, a tree twisted and hoary with lichen and without a red berry among its spineless leaves. The holly grew near a mountain ash. Both had been palnted by birds.

Looking down, while holding a branch of holly, Seventy-Six could see the toff kneeling by the girl and below them, the river at the base of the hill. He neither saw nor heard hounds, for they were running down the unseen slope which led from the marshy ground. Beyond the marsh, on the opposite hillock, was the badger holt.

He climbed the clitter, and went at a steady pace onwards. Here was drier ground that dipped gradually to a saucer-like depression rising to Links Tor about a mile away against the sky. Being under the everlasting wind the heather was knee-deep and springy. There were no rocks to hinder. The flagpole on Hare Tor to the south—erected to give the signal when gunners were firing on the artillery ranges—lost its dark outline in a drift of cloud as he started to ascend again.

Seventy-Six began to hear the wind as he climbed towards Links Tor. From a sighing in the stalks of heather it swelled to a chilly whistling, and his clothes were blown against his form. About fifty yards from the summit, where was lodged a squat roundish mass of black granite grooved and scalloped and smoothed by wind and rain of a thousand centuries, he sat down and rested. Turning in a northerly direction he saw a great brown and grey ball of a hill, at whose base ran the leaden vein of the Lyd. He looked across the Great Nodden to fields in sunlight and shadow, and away to a blue infinity of land and sky. The south was dim and grey. Rain. Seventy-Six was glad, for it would hide him. He thought that he would strike inland to the moor behind him and hide till dusk, when he would return and make for the sea. As he became hopeful again he felt sorry that he had slung the brick at that young toff. It had been done in fear.

A sudden deep croaking over his shoulder made him turn his head. He was in time to see black cartwheeling wings as a bird swerved and dropped out of sight behind the tor again. The raven had meant to alight there, but something had disturbed it. As Seventy-Six stared he saw a thin object, like a stick, thrust up from the centre of the granite. It thickened towards its end, and then it disappeared. In its place was an arm, followed by a head and shoulders. A man then levered himself upon the platform, picked up a rifle, and staggered to his feet, his legs crooked as he braced himself against the blast of the wind.

Seventy-Six tried to force his head back to its normal position, but it was held there as though by a spring fixed to his spine. He continued to stare at the crooked figure on

Links Tor. He had to stiffen the muscles of throat and neck before he could force his head away. He sat rigidly, wondering when he would be shot in the back. He waited, until the feeling in his spine compelled him to twist his head again. The warder had dropped on one knee, and was covering the convict with his rifle.

Seventy-Six pretended not to have seen him. The curiosity of dread made him turn round once more, just as a shout enfeebled by wind came from the warder. He was beckoning Seventy-Six, standing as upright as the wind would permit, and holding the rifle in his right hand at the position of trail. Seventy-Six got on his feet, and while he was walking towards the tor, the warden pulled a whistle from his breast pocket and blew a long blast. As though in answer a ragged edge of mist trailed in cold silence past the convict, and washed around the monolith of granite. Links Tor faded out, but the whistle continued its double note—*fran-n-n-n* in the fog.

5

Seventy-Six stood irresolute. He felt for the head of the pin. The touch of its head was like a double dose of rum before going over the bags. He laughed, and was turning it in finger and thumb when a hound spoke below. It was the leader, a dog named Lamplight. The pack was less than a mile away, running the line of the yellow boots, whose scent was pungent in the mist. Again Seventy-Six thought of being caned on his hands, before the boys and girls of the fifth standard of the Council School. He remembered the bag of aniseed balls, which he had been made to throw in the master's waste-paper basket—his mother's birthday gift, bought with one of her scanty spare pennies. And afterwards the master had made him face the class, and had used the little boy's tearful gulping for a crudely sarcastic lecture on the subject of Heroism. He had not known that a son felt that his mother's heart was thrown in the basket.

Seventy-six thought, This fog is a bit of all right! Stuff to give the troops! He set off at a run, on his toes. He had been the champion runner of his battalion. The moor was a chaos of whitey-grey, cold and dim. Soon his eyelashes were damp. The ground was firm, and he leapt over the ling. The rubber pads gave a good grip. After a quarter of an hour his breath came quickly, and he felt a relief when the ground began to slope down. The noise of water was before him. Lower and lower he descended until he came to the Rattlebrook fretting its stony bed. He crossed without wetting his feet, and listened. In front of him the ground rose again, and a remote baying seemed to float down through the mist. He pushed on up the hill, but was forced to rest at the top. He imagined that as he was invisible, he was safe, because he did not know that hounds followed by nose alone. As he lay on a couch of ling he heard them giving tongue, not an echo this time. They had reached the unseen crest of the coombe. He jumped up and hastened onwards, cursing them because he thought they would betray him to the warders. The clamour suddenly increased—where Seventy-Six had rested—and he ran on again.

His next rest was half an hour later, when he flung himself by a thread of a stream which had cut for itself a channel in the peaty soil. He dipped his hat in the brown water, flinging it over his face and washing out his mouth. In the old running days, when the Guards Division had been out of the line, he had been trained never to drink before or during a long-distance run. He lay on his back, wishing he had a pal with him; one minute, two minutes, three minutes, and then the baying of hounds.

Patches of ling and grass tufts became scantier. Everywhere was water. The rubber soles of his boots often slid. He ran flat-footed over a maze of water-threads. An idea came to him that he must jump them all, that he would have bad luck if he slipped into one. To ease himself he carried the hat in his left hand. It began to impede him, but he dared not throw it away, as he would need it until his hair grew. It hindered more when carried under an arm, so he rammed it on his head again. During the next half hour, toiling up a long hill, he changed its position more than a dozen times.

Eventually the hat was thrown away beside a layer of turves that had been cut and laid in wide arrow-shaped lines to drain and dry, where it was found long afterwards. Disturbed in their feeding, three golden plover rose in the mist before the runner with swift anchor-winged flight and with gentle cries of alarm. Snipe, thrusting long bills into the soft ground, were driven up from their feeding. Sometimes a raven croaked over his head.

He was so fatigued when he reached the Great Knesset that he had to walk. His feet, with blistered toes and heels, felt as hot and heavy as they had felt when he had trench-feet swelled and red as tomatoes. He flung away the stolen shirt, soggy with sweat, on the morass where the river Tavy rises. His trousers to the knees were wet and black with peat. He had blundered into many shallow bogs. The deep sucking quakers, which shook and rippled at his passing, were bright green and easily seen.

He staggered across the plash in the peaty hollow of an old tarn, hid by swirls of fog. A broken spade was stuck into a heap of turves in the hollow, and in the turves was an iron box holding a metal stamp, a bottle of violet ink, and a book wherein many names were signed. Its fly-leaf was ringed and smudged by intersecting violet circles holding the letters CRANMERE. Seventy-Six remembered. Past and present were mingled as reality in his confused brain. In the early summer of 1914 a London-born youth and his wife, on their honeymoon, had scrawled their names across a page, with the remark, *It's all rite*. And no, nearly ten years later, the mortal remains of the woman mould-ered in a South London graveyard and neither age nor name mattered further for the husband. Seventy-Six, grey-haired, was resting the weight of his head and shoulders on forehead and knees; but a younger man, in khaki, was writing a letter to a wife still living: *Dear Dol, i write hoping you are quite all rite, as it leaves me at present, in the pink. Are you getting the seperation allowance all rite. I hopes so. We are not allowed to say where we are but it isn't so bad, although a bit of mud about. I hope to get Blighty leaf soon it is my turn soon and i hops the Sarjint Major don't forgit. No more now from your lovin husband Bob.*

P.S. This war is a Bastard.

He blacked out the last word, remembering that his officer would read the letter.

And SWAK on the envelope flap—Sealed With A Kiss. The pencil-stump, paper, and sand-bagged traverse, sun shining, plank he sat on, all dropped into darkness. He heard the whining of ricochets, saw the greenish flares quivering in the water-filled shell-holes as the relieved right-wing company filed down the wooden track to the Menin Road. Jerry's machine guns were clacking from many points. Going out at last! Rest billets reached, and rum-in-tea dished out. The S.M. was calling out names for Blighty leaf. Christ, 'ow 'is 'eart thumped! 'Is own number, 'is name! He saw again the lorry in which he had hopped to railhead, after fourteen months in the mud of Artois and the shallow water trenches of the Salient. During the slow journey in the train, clanking and stopping and jerking on again past sandhills and pines to Boulogne, the young Coalie was singing and shouting, happy at the thought of seeing again the wife he had constantly thought of, but infrequently written to, during so many evenings in smoky estaminets, candle-dim billets, and lousy cubbie-holes. A stay of two days in the rest camp owing to submarines in the Channel, and again he was singing with his chums as they marched down the quay. Horse-nosed officer bloke with A.M.L.O. on his brassard, at the gangway with red-cap sergeant and two policemen scrutinizing the yellow pass. Then the pitch and roll of the boat, the nausea and prostration, the grey cliffs of England, the pulling-himself-together and the tottering off at Folkestone, the train with the black-painted lamps and drawn blinds, the faces in smoke and the crush of equipment, the glide into Victoria Station so vast and dark and subdued, yet noisy with feet and engine steam. Outside the women he didn't want to talk to saying, "Hullo, dearie," and then—the first drink of good old English beer, a pint of mild-and-bitter . . . How strange civvy suits looked!

One reality faded; nausea remained. Seventy-Six lifted his head and harkened to hounds following him in the mist. Two hours before they had streamed over the ragged grass below Links Tor. They were unfatigued, but had veered off the line, following the aniseed straying in the mist. Seventy-Six thought that the warders would see his name in the book, and know that he had been past Cranmere. He carried the book away with him, and trod it into a bog, where it was never found . . . afterwards it was indignantly stated that someone had taken it because it contained the autograph of the Prince of Wales.

6

Seventy-Six loped on for another half-hour, descending to a coombe where the mist was thinner. He fell over a rock beside a stream, and choked as he tried to suck up water which turned his teeth to icicles. When he tried to rise again he had to draw his feet from off the rock; he felt as though he were dragging the rock with them. He prayed with broken shouts, as he had prayed under the barrage at Festubert. His ribs were hugging him to death, the prison shirt was smothering him. He tore it off and left it on the rock, and pulled himself onwards, as a child in a night-

mare. Now he was clad only in trousers and boots, and the
Union Jack tattooed on his back. The flag was one of the
patriotic relics of 1914, done in a Caterham shop after
cheers and beers with pals, following flaring mental hatred
of the sergeant-instructor drilling the squad to breaking
point on the parade ground.

Over rocks and rushy tufts, while thirty-four hounds
followed less than three hundred yards behind. His line of
running had been in a loop, and he was approaching the
Rattlebrook again, where it merged into the yellow winter
water of the Tavy. He plunged into the river foaming and
swirling among black and pink-blotched boulders and
rocky tables, which for centuries the floods had slowly
carved. It sucked him under and spun him in its twist. A
spur of rock held him by the trousers, until they ripped,
and wrapped round his legs. Hauling himself out,
Seventy-Six waded back into the river again when the
leading hounds viewed him and gave tongue.

He was carried a hundred yards down the water in less
than a minute, to where a tree-grown islet divided the
current. All the air was knocked from his chest. On hands
and knees he crawled to the right bank. The strings of his
thigh and calf muscles were drawn tight, and each lung
was bayoneted. A spike of rock had torn his back, and the
Union Jack was fouled by the blood of the ruined patriot.

A mist strayed through Tavy Cleave, and the broken
screes towering hundreds of feet above were revealed and
hidden by clouds. An old hill-fox deep in a clitter sniffed as
he passed below and listened contentedly to the hounds
which had crossed the river. The raven that had observed
Seventy-Six for nearly three hours croaked a treble croak
to its mate from a scaur of rock four hundred feet above the
toiling figure.

It was now between half-past two and three o'clock in
the afternoon. Feeling for the pin, Seventy-Six realized
that he had thrown it away with the clothes.

Ever since he had been blown by a high-explosive shell

out of a communication trench in the Hohenzollern Redoubt, with burst sandbags and pieces of a shattered Coalie, his chum, a spectre had fretted his life. Always—and especially in drink—since his fourteen days in the hospital of Hazebrouck 'recovering' from the shock of the bright shell-blast, he had been liable to moods both morose and violent. At Hazebrouck an inspecting Surgeon-General, a regular officer with two rows of ribbons and honours, suspected him of malingering, and ordered him immediately to be sent back to duty in the line.

The thought of his wife had kept the spectre away; as afterwards, the companionship of the pin in his cell had been a barrier against the dark fears which came into his poor disrupted mind. When he knew that the pin was lost, Seventy-Six threw up his arms and wailed. He saw what other men would not have seen, had they been with him. The new consciousness was accompanied by a sense of ease and lightness. All pain and fatigue left him. He seemed to be floating along, with the least touch of his toes on rocks and water.

The body of Seventy-Six was hobbling in the smooth and shallow bed of the leat which, serpentining through the moor, eventually brought water for use in the arsenic mines of Mary Tavy; but a Coldstream Guardsman also was walking on the platform of the Tube Railway at the Elephant and Castle Station. The platform was thick with the smell of many women and children sitting and lying against the wall. He was relieved that the journey was finished, and hitching up rifle on right shoulder he shoved a way into the lift. Outside the dear old boozer, where he had first met his wife. Now there was a war on, and a bloke couldn't get a pint after nine o'clock. The street was dark. A tramcar passed him, bumping and clattering, all its lights blacked over, except for the least glimmers. He lit a cigarette, and the voice of a special contable riding past on a lampless bicycle cried out in agitated sternness: *Put that light out! Second warning's been given!* He answered with a laugh, *Don't get the wind up, mate!* As he strode along the Old Kent Road, gunfire broke out, and a hundred white beams swept the sky. The yelling civvies might cut and run, but not a Coalie! He whistled as he walked. *Z-z-z-z-zim-z-zz-zop* fell the splinters of anti-aircraft shells. *Wh-oo-sh! Crack!* that was a nosecap that had split the paving stone just behind him. He walked on to his street, erect and with cap-peak pulled low over his eyes. Near his house he stopped and looked upwards. A groaning had opened in the sky above him. It filled the street, it snored gigantically through the darkness. *Whooursh, whooursh*, an immense slow corkscrewing of sound, that grew as though the earth was falling out of its orbit. The soldier crouched under a window ledge, while a starving cat miaowed to him, and rubbed itself against his cheek. Poor moggy, he 'adn't no milk to give. He stroked the cat, whose purring was drowned in the tremendous rushing noise descending. It was like a thousand minnies coming down. (The minenwerfen in the Salient had made a lesser noise.) He waited and sweated, for it was coming straight at him. He pressed himself against the wall, against the bricks made greasy by children's hands, holding the cat protected in his arms, his eyes closed, his breath stopped. A red glare showed through his lids, and immediately a stunning detonation flung him with the cat into the gutter. Houses swayed and tumbled and roared down in clouds of bricks and dust. He ran up the street, for the Zeppelin torpedo had fallen just about where he lived. The bomb had flattened a row of houses, but his house was safe, except for a splintered door. Won't Old Dol be surprised to see me, he thought, jubilant that he was still alive. He pushed the door down, crashing in upon the landlady, an old widow woman who was wearing a crimson flannel nightgown. Her bluish-white face was beyond speech. She moaned something, and pointed at a broken methylated spirit bottle on the floor. *Where's Doll?* he asked, *Upstairs?* She stood and moaned in the crude fumes of her own breath. *You're boozed, Ma!* he said. She let out a shriek when he pointed upstairs. *I to'd her not to do it! I to'd 'er not to!* she moaned. Her candle wobbled and fell. He ran up the stairs, pulling himself up with his hands and stones out of the wall fell away with his clutch. (Seventy-Six had reached the ruin of Redford Farm.) He turned the handle of the bed-sitting-room. The door was locked. A man's voice said, *What the bleedin' 'ell.* With the butt of his rifle he broke in the panels, and burst the lock. A gas jet burned with a small blue flame. The soldier turned the tap, and it flittered like a yellow bat. He snarled and drew his bayonet out of the scabbard, and fixed it. The man whined, *'Ere, I say, maite, what's the bleedin' gaine?* Then he shrieked and hid his face under the bedclothes, with the soldier's wife. The soldier stabbed them under the patched counterpane. He saw the spirit of his wife fly up on white wings. (The owl flew out of the chimney of Redford Farm.) But the bloke she had picked up wouldn't die. After each lunge of the bayonet he came alive again with more and more faces, which tried to bite him with their fangs. The soldier thrust and pointed, *groin—belly—right nipple—left nipple—throat—in—out—on guard!* Just as the sergeant-instructor had yelled at him during bayonet practice on the stuffed sacks at Caterham. He smashed with the butt-stroke on their jaws and eyes, but the faces pulled him down. He did not care, they did not hurt him, and with a laugh he felt himself withdrawn from them, into darkness.

7

Redford Farm, near the leat which leads to the arsenic mines, had been a ruin many years before the last run of the Inclefell Harriers. One chimney-stack was still standing at the eastern end of the farmhouse the Saturday before, for on that day, wandering over the moor, the young man who was the guest of the squire of Lydford had disturbed a white owl that was dozing away the daylight up the flue, among the fire-marked stones. But on the Monday, when Miss Mollie Inclefell, lost in the mist for some hours, and leading her mare lame in the near fore, arrived at Redford Farm about three o'clock, it had collapsed, as though someone had tried to climb up it. A raven flew over the heap of stones and damp mortar-dust lying on the ground. Several red-muzzled hounds came to her and leapt up affectionately. They remained by her, two of them licking her face, while she lay pale and still in a fainting fit caused by the sight of two shinbones sticking out of a pair of yellow boots.

CRIME AND PUNISHMENT

This is the story of a dog called Snapper—a good name for him—and an American gentleman who lived for a month or two in Devon, on the funds provided by a travelling research scholarship. The Assistant Professor went to Devon with the idea of writing a history of the French Revolution.

Our story opens one fine May morning, when the Assistant Professor of Comparative Literature—to give him his proper style and title—looked out of his study window and cursed. In the middle of the lawn below was a small circular flower-bed, out of which grew a cypress tree. It was not the sight of the tree that caused annoyance, but the fact, as it appeared to him, that it was rapidly being dug up.

In fact the tree had stood there for a couple of hundred years or more, the age of the digger was scarcely half a couple of hundred days, and the hole was not more than a foot deep and about five inches wide. Nevertheless, a shower of earth was descending upon the lawn.

The Assistant Professor pushed open the casement and bawled, "Hey, Snapper! Grr, you! Go some place else, go kill real rats! Where did that darned woman put the soda? I guess the farmer's pork is all nobs and gas inside me." He patted his waistcoat with mournful self-sympathy. "Jeese, I wish I had the dog's outlook on life," he said to himself. "He doesn't trouble about the French Revolution."

The soil which had been increasing for the past few minutes between the hind legs of the terrier ceased to heave; a head and ears dishevelled with earth were withdrawn, and the thing called Snapper wagged its tail once, uncertainly. It turned its earthy face to the window, laid back its long ears, and showed its teeth in a grin.

"Naughty boy!" said the Assistant Professor, in a tone of voice that caused the back of the puppy to straighten, its ears and tail-stump to become vertical. "Mustn't dig up other folks' trees! The British author I rent the house from will sock me for dilapidations, although strictly speaking it should be deracinations, except that the word deracination doesn't occur in my lease. Mind you don't wag that tail right off, Snapper. Go play with that bull again. I'll try and take you for a walk this afternoon. Goo' boy, Snapper! Jeese, you're a cheerful little guy. What a lot of kicks you get out of life!"

The puppy was now running round the lawn at its fastest pace, round and round the cypress tree. At speed its hair was pressed against its body, and it seemed to have enormous black eyebrows.

"Wish I could feel like you do," said the Assistant Professor. "I guess it's an illusion to grade you a lower species just because your ears are long and hiary, and you run on four legs and catch your fleas without mental poise and philosophical detachment. Wal, there you are enjoying yourself in the sunshine, never needing soda after your meals, without giving a darn why you are or who you are, and here am I, sitting day after day writing a lot of bunk about something that probably never happened among a lot of cockaded cok-eyed morons nearly a hundred and fifty years ago. Wait till I've broken the back of this chapter on Talleyrand, Snapper, then I'll take you for a walk this afternoon, a real walk."

The assistant Professor went back to his chair and stared gloomily at the mass of books and papers cluttering the desk.

2

Left alone, the puppy lifted his nose and sniffed the air for an interesting smell. He was at that stage of his self-education when the allurements of reality and imagination were almost equal. No interesting smells being on the air, he began to imagine a colony of rats at the end of the hole under the cypress. He was about to dig for them when the scent of his favourite cat set across his nostrils. Up went his tail and ears.

A few moments later he saw the cat walking with slow unconcern up the rose path on its way to the kitchen door and the dustbin. He rushed forward jubilantly. The cat fluffed herself, flattened her ears, opened her claws, and spat. Snapper barked with joy. Very soon he had man-oeuvred her to his favourite pitch at the edge of the lawn. He pranced before her, darting left and right, making feints forward and then springing back. She lay under the edge of the lawn on the path, showing only her moving tail-tip and her flattened ears. *Waugh waugh waugh!* Then occurred what Snapper had been deliriously awaiting: the cat sprang and struck at him. Snapper, feeling very clever, nimbly avoided her clip. She clawed the grass, and after a baffled hiss, chased him round the tree.

Snapper was so happy that he ran round the tree three times after the cat had retired to her base on the path at the edge of the lawn. To the left and to right he pranced again, defying her, baring his teeth at her, feinting forward, always alert to dodge the sudden lunge and hook of claws.

Glad of the excuse to quit the pangs of writing a masterpeice, the Assistant Professor looked down at them from his window. Then he saw the farmer, whose horrid pork was resisting every assault of the Assistant Professor's gastric juices, walking up the garden path.

The terrier raised its long bat-like ears, uttered a bark, and trotted to meet the farmer.

In one hand the farmer held a dead pullet by its yellow legs. Snapper nosed the bird and leapt up, uttering a gurgling growl of delight. The farmer grunted, knocked it against the terrier's head, and growled "Get off, you limmer! Next time I catch you nosing round my shed, you'll get something you aren't expecting. That's the second bird you've had in one day, you bissley li'l beggar!"

"Good morning!" the Professor called from the window, in an English accent. Then reverting to his native Connecticut, "Hello, has my darned dog been at your chickens again? Just a minute, I'll be right down!"

Five minutes afterwards the farmer was returning down the garden path, and the Assistant Professor, a methodical, industrious and ambitious young man, was entering in his *Diary of Work in Progress, Europe,* under the heading *Incidental Expenses*, the item:

One chicken, bought from Whiskers   4*s*.
Six weeks before, there had been this entry:
One pedigree Jack Russell terrier, bought from
Henry Williamson   £5 5*s*. 0*d*.

3

That afternoon the Assistant Professor sat in his study, groaning, forcing the pen slowly across the paper. Six weeks of his vacation were gone, and he had not yet got half-way through his schedule, which was to bring him to Chapter Eighty of Volume Four of *An Historical Outline of the French Revolution.* He had been working on his masterpiece for more than ten years. For more than ten years the Assistant Professor had been reading every available book already published on the subject; for more than ten years he had been reading, and reviewing for various highbrow literary weeklies, every new book on the subject published in the U.S. When one highbrow literary weekly folded, the Professor continued to review for its successor, until that died, and then he went after the next one. During the ten years he had fairly established within himself the idea that he was *the* American authority on how not to write about the French Revolution. Every book on the French Revolution reviewed by the Assistant Professor was discovered to be deficient in this or that aspect of behaviourism, faulty in this or that interpretation of psychological or character motivation. This book, or that book, declared the reviewer, was not the comprehensive masterpiece that was awaited by the world, the masterpiece that would reveal the decline and fall of idealism in the light of modern knowledge, that would transcend even Thomas Carlyle. A few highballs helped to clarify, now and again, the essential urgency of his own mission in the matter of writing *the* definite *opus* on the French Revolution.

Nevertheless, in spite of deficiencies in aspects of behaviourism and faults in interpretation of psychological or character motivation, every new book on the French Revolution added a weight to the appalling mass of material, to be worked into the comprehensive masterpiece awaited by the world, which accompanied the Assistant Professor everywhere; a mass, which at the moment when the Professor bought a pullet for twice its market value, filled three immense trunks and weighed over a quarter of a ton.

If this awful fact, and what it signifies, has not already flattened the reader of this little story, please be reassured immediately: pray remain seated: in a moment or two you will be watching the little dog, who waited in vain for its promised walk, playing with its friend the bull. You'll hear only once more of the manuscript of *An Historical Outline of the French Revolution*, which with its five hundred pound of parasites was only dragged in to show how, in spite of his modern way of talking, the Assistant Professor was really a very cultured person. So while with

weary determination he is digging into one of his several
trunks, among the moths and mildew, in order to verify
and embody—away with culture, the word is pinch—in
order to pinch a few facts from one of the old review copies
therein, come on tip-toe beside me, and watch the tech-
nique of Snapper with the bull.

4

The bull does not want to play with any silly little dog. He
is a young bull, but recently separated from his mother the
Aberdeen-Angus pedigree cow, all of whose milk he has
sucked during the first eight months of his life. He is
square, almost, when seen from behind; and the line of his
back is straight. Shoulders all beef. He is what is called
polled; he has no horns. Which is perhaps as well for
Snapper; who anyway, would not care. Was he not descended from a line of fierce and eager little earth-dogs,
bred to tackle badger and fox underground? The bull is
standing in the shade of a beech tree as Snapper trots
to within two yards of him. Snapper crouches in the grass.

The bull turns his head, with its curly black poll, and
stares at the white crouching object with the bright eyes.
Snapper makes his ears cock—or rather, he makes them
stand up straight, for they are too ludicrously tall for the
action to be called cocking—and lies still in the grass,
taunting the bull to play.

"*Humph!*" says the bull, and swishes his tail.

"*Worro-worro-wough!*" replies Snapper, making a sort of
amiable growling in his throat. The bull slowly turns
away his head, and gives an extra flick to his tail. Snapper
leaps up, and runs round to face him, collapsing in the
grass again. The bull bends his neck and gently lifts his
nose, with the copper ring, in the direction of the dog.

"*Worro-worro,*" growls Snapper, with delight. He runs

to and fro before the bull several times, before collapsing in the grass, pointing himself at the bull with shining eyes, inviting him to lower his head so that he, Snapper, may have the pleausre of springing away from the thrilling snort of his nostril.

The bull turns away.

Snapper barks. Raucousness is now in his voice. The bull does not want to play, so Snapper runs twistedly at the bull, showing his eye-teeth in a grin, and snapping a couple of inches away from the bull's muzzle. *Wough wough!*

The bull glares and snorts.

"*Ha ha!*" pants Snapper, prancing. "*Wough wough!*" He runs at the bull again, leaping aside, falling over, wriggling quickly upright, and making a circle away from his glaring friend the enemy.

So happy is Snapper that he dashes round the bull half a dozen times, before crouching again at the challenge. The bull paws the ground, and pretends to graze.

Snapper, after several feints in the grass, then threatens the bull by pushing himself on his belly towards him. To lure the bull he gets up again, shakes himself, and pretends to stare at a pigeon flying over. He yawns, making a plaintive sound. Nothing happens.

The bull crops, or pretends to crop, at a tuft of rank marsh-grass, which cattle never eat. Snapper walks behind him, collapses to scratch himself, then suddenly runs in and nips the idly swinging tail at its tuft.

The bull swings round, snorting, and paws the ground. Snapper barks, crouches on his forepaws. The bull trots forward with lowered head. His eyes gleam as he runs at the dog.

Snapper flees swiftly. Only when he has scrambled under the gate does he face the bull. Very bravely he thrusts his head between the lower bars and snarls a challenge. The bull has scared him.

"*Poof!*" snorts the bull, jarring the gate with his curly

brow. Snapper nips his nose, not hard, but enough to make the bull swish his tail violently. The bull holds up his head, preparing to shut his eyes and to toss gate and dog over his back. *Crash! Crack!* Snapper turns tail and flees silently.

"Aa-ah-you," roars the farmer, coming down the hedge, and hearing the splintering of the lower bar of the gate. "You young limmer, you! Wait till I get near enough to put my stick about 'ee! Go after something your own size, why don't 'ee?" he yells after the dog. "Go and kill some of the ould rats round the stables!"

The small white dog, its long black ears raised in alarm, rapidly vanishes.

Amusing little cove, isn't he?

5

As soon as he was out of sight of the farmer Snapper stopped and rolled luxuriously in the grass. Something very nice and sweet-smelling lay in the grass. He had rolled on it many time before. During several weeks he had played with it, shaking and tearing with rage; but now the feeling he had for it was quite different. Of course there are, in the U.S.A., canine psychologists, whose work precedes that of the genii who inhabit the Halls of Memory, of Doggy Delight, wherein pets are embalmed, stuffed, and otherwise preserved in the Happy Hunting Grounds of Eternity, Inc. Without doubt, a doctor of that school of canine psychology would gravely have pronounced, Snapper has a manic-depressive complex. Was it caused by some fixation in early life? the Professor might have inquired, some dread shock in whelphood? Certainly the dog had bad dreams, wherein his legs and nose worked agitatedly and his ears rose and fell like English railway signals at the end of a prolonged fog.

Snapper is the first morbid dog in fiction: definitely he had the Cadaver Complex, or maybe the Dingo Complex: for he delighted to roll on the flattened corpse of a rat.

After rolling for several minutes, he arose, shook himself, inspected the corpse, performed a thoughtful ceremony upon it, and trotted off. He had recalled one of the sounds issuing from the farmer—*rats*.

6

The farmer at this period was much troubled by rats. His farm was near a hunting stables. Recently some of the stable buildings had been improved. Rickety wooden bins for oats and bran and other food had been replaced by modern bins of galvanised iron. The rats which had grown numerous and fat on plundered corn were now shut out. Their runs and highways had been stopped with wads of wire netting rammed into the holes, and the floor covered with concrete. A determined rat might eventually gnaw through concrete, unless it were made of granite chip, but the sharp points of wire defeated them. So they migrated to the farm.

Snapper had spent much time in digging and blowing and snuffling and whining in the farmer's wood shed, his long ears stiff with excitement, but only in dreams had he got his teeth across one.

As he went towards the farmyard he forgot the rats, for he saw his friends the fifteen pigs. At least, Snapper must have considered them his friends, for he always ran gleefully towards them when he saw them; but it is doubtful if the pigs thought of him as their friend. One of them, however, the sow, who weighed about a quarter of a ton, definitely regarded Snapper as her friend.

They were all pink. Their family name was Long White Lopeared Pig. Snapper made two discriminations among

them: one was much bigger than the others, and unplay-
able; the other was much smaller than the rest, and could
be rolled over in the mud squealing. This wretched individual was the smallest of the farrow, his head was too big
and his body too small, and only laziness on the farmer's
part had prevented him from being killed at birth. A
'nestledraff', as farmers called this oddment, would make
neither pork nor bacon. In the farmer's words, he 'ate more
than the head o'n was worth'. Even so, the poor nestledraff ate little enough, always being squeezed out in the
scramble. He was Snapper's favourite, for Snapper could
do what he liked with him. He could pull the little crea-
ture's tail, nip his ears and jowl and nose, chase him all
through the midden, and roll him on his back in the muck.

Play with it, however, did not usually last very long,
because what Snapper really liked was a fight, or what to
him was a fight. The larger pigs would run and dodge him
for a while, and then stand still looking at him from
between their ears. This gave Snapper a thrill, for when
they stood like that they were ready to snap at him. Then
he could dance around on his toes. As for the lumbering
sow, she grunted and snuffled about the farmyard, and
took no heed of him. She had long given up hope of any
excitement from his presence. Once Snapper had rolled by
accident off an empty barrel lying on its side outside the
farmhouse door, and fallen sprawling on her back, in the
precise place where she needed to be scratched. He had not
known that the sow's grunts were of pleasure; he had been
wary of her long snout ever since.

Snapper had been playing with the piglets, causing
squeaks and grunts and sudden patterings in the mud, for
about ten minutes, and was in the act of pulling the curl out
of a pink tail, when he was startled by a gruff voice
shouting terribly near:

"Ah, you'm here again, be 'ee? Well, I like your bliddy
cheek! Go on, out of it!" the farmer bellowed, his red face
working. "Us'll be seeing master, soon, to get 'ee a good

trimming. You'll come here once too often, my little boy, and find yourself looking at the wrong end of my gun!"

The farmer held another dead chicken in his hand. Nearly all its breast feathers had been torn off, and it was bitten in many places. Snapper fled.

The howls of a dog being trimmed came from the Assistant Professor's hired house. Afterwards the dead fowl was solemnly fastened by string to the dog's neck. The Professor hurled a stick into the hedge. "Remember—'ware feather, Snapper!" he intoned solemnly, in an Englishman's sporting voice: adding, "Gee, I'm sorry, but I've got to do it."

Shortly afterwards an entry was made under the heading *Incidental Expenses* in the *Diary of Work in Progress, Europe*:

One chicken, bought from Whiskers   5s.

7

The Assistant Professor stood by the window of the study. Papers, books, pens, pipes, and cigarette ends were everywhere. He addressed the woebegone figure of the dog sitting under the cypress tree below.

"Morally speaking, I ought to be wearing the darned thing next my gullet," he soliloquised. "Let me get the back of this chapter broken, then I'll take you walks."

Hearing the voice Snapper looked up, and wagged his tail. Whereupon the voice said sternly, "'Ware feather, Snapper! 'Ware fether! Isn't that the correct Britisher's admonition? 'Ware feather, Snapper! Poor little devil, you're all fire and fun, and no one to play with. Wait till I've gotten rid of this moron Mirabeau, then we'll have some swell walks right across Exmoor. Meanwhile— 'ware feather, Snapper!"

Snapper watched the window for a few minutes after

master had disappeared, and then stared about him, wondering what to do. He sighed, and tried half-heartedly to play with the chicken slung around his neck; but it did not respond, and he thought he would sleep.

At that moment his favourite cat, one of half a dozen that lived in the barns and sheds of the farm, walked across the lawn, on its way to the dustbin. Immediately his ears stood up. He ran at her, but the weight attached to his collar made him stumble and fall over. Instantly the cat pounced, bit him through the ear, got in several pleasing rips with her hind legs on his back, spat at him, smacked him on the nose as he struggled up yelping, then fled, leaving him to walk slowly back to his hole under the cypress, wondering why he had been hurt. He tried to lick his nose, and in doing so got tangled up with the chicken.

Hearing the yelp, the Assistant Professor flung down the pen he had been gnawing, got up, and walked to the window. He was in time to see Snapper, as he thought, trying to eat the chicken. That would never do! It was intended that the dog should drag about his victim for two days, becoming so humiliated, so sick of chicken that he would never look at another one in his life; but if Snapper were treating it as a joke . . .

"'Ware feather, Snapper!" bellowed the Professor.

"Aiy aiy!" cried the voice of the farmer, who was hastening up the garden path. "You'm just in time with your advice sir!" Indignantly he held up the corpse of a third chicken.

"Well, I'm darned," said the Professor. He thought a moment. "But surely the dog has not had time to go around to your place and come back here again. Why, I've scarcely had time to write a sentence between the time of licking him and tying that chicken round his neck, and this your third visit."

"I'm very sorry, sir," said the farmer, "but here's my poult, bootiful little bird it be, too, and there, if you'll please to look, be the marks of worrying, identical with the marks on the other poults. If you'll please to step down a minute, sir, I'll show 'ee. Ah, you may well cringe!" he growled to Snapper, who was creeping off in a sidling walk, ears down, body curved, his tail–stump nervously fluttering.

"Come here, sir!" shouted the Professor. Snapper turned on his back, held his pointed nose up as though he were trying to smell a cloud in the sky, and waited for inevitable pain.

Together the Assistant Professor and the farmer compared the marks on the fresh chicken with those of the bedraggled thing attached to the dog. Snapper, lying on his back, looked first at one face, then at the other, anxiously awaiting their verdict. His eyes, under the black eyebrows, rolled, showing the whites, as he watched master going towards that part of the hedge where the stick had been flung. Master returned with the stick. Snapper sprang up, meaning to run away and hide in the new hole he had been excavating in the coal–shed, but he was handicapped by the weight round his neck. Master caught him and whacked him, and as Snapper crept away into the hedge with both ears pressed flat on his skull, the farmer said, putting five shillings and sixpence into his pocket:

"Well, thank you, sir, I don't want to raise trouble, but I'm a poor man and I've got my living to make. The price be market price for growing birds, which put on a lot of flesh at this season o' the year, sir."

"The law of supply and demand has always puzzled me," said the Professor. "But at least I see quite clearly that as the supply diminishes so the value increases. Say, I've an idea. Why not let me buy the remaining pullets from you now at five shillings each. Then those that Snapper doesn't want, I'll sell back to you at the end of the month for what I pay for them now."

"Thank you, sir, I'm sure, but who'll be paying for their food meanwhile?"

"Jeese, I guess you've got me licked," said the Profes-

sor. "I understand why all revolutions are bound to fail.
I'll have to keep Snapper tied up, that's all. Good
afternoon."

The Professor returned to his study, and made a further
entry into his diary of expenses.

Further contribution to the chicken racket   5s. 6d.

"The horney old buzzard," he muttered. "And he took
the durned thing away with him, too!"

After walking round the room several times and trying
to light a pipe that was too tightly packed, the Assistant
Professor sat down at his desk once more. To his surprise
and delight his pen began to move over the paper rapidly,
in pursuit of a scathing criticism of French peasantry, small
farmers, and all bourgeoisie. Page after page he filled with
what he felt to be a brilliantly argued plea for the necessity
of authoritarianism. At last he ceased, and looking at his
watch was astonished to see that nearly two hours had
elapsed. He had forgotten all about Snapper! Anyhow,
now he could take the dog for a walk with a clear
conscience.

He went downstairs into the garden and was about to
whistle for the puppy-dog when from the farmyard across
the lane he heard the roar of the farmer's voice, followed
by two shots and the high yelping of a dog.

Clenching his fists, the Assistant Professor ran in the
direction of the farmyard.

8

Now after the second thrashing, the trembling Snapper
had remained in the hedge. But soon one of his ears had
raised itself, and he yawned. Gazing around, he smelled
nothing to do. He arose and shook himself. Then he
walked away, dragging the cold thing beside him, and sat

for a while under the holly bush by the kitchen door. He watched the cat eating the remains of his dinner, without even uttering one growl of querulous protest. Having licked the plate clean, the cat then sat beside it and thoroughly washed his face and paws, watched by the shivering Snapper, who had curled himself on an uneasy bed of dead holly leaves, his head pillowed on the thing which was fastened to him. Having completed her leisurely toilet, the cat got up and walked back towards the farmhouse. Snapper then walked over and woefully inspected the empty plate. He yawned, stretched himself, and trotted back to the cypress tree, animated by the thought of digging out imaginary rats.

Encumbered by the dead weight round his neck, he soon grew tired, and collapsing into the hole, went to sleep. Sometimes he whined in his sleep, dreaming of master chasing him with a stick as big as master, the end of which was a cat's paw with great curved claws, master and cat's-paw always just behind his tail however hard he tried to race away, and although he was running his fastest, he was not moving, and although he was not moving, the terrible cat's-paw never actually struck him.

With relief Snapper awoke from this nightmare, and looked about him, shivering. Master's window was blank. He heard sounds of distant pigs grunting, cows lowing, hens clucking, but they excited no desire in him. He curled into a tighter circle, settled his head across his paws, swallowed the water in his mouth, sighed with contentment that he was not really being beaten but was saftely tucked into his retreat, and went to sleep again.

As the Assistant Professor was writing the last of his indictment (which was scrapped that same evening, for reasons that soon will be apparent) Snapper awoke, remembered his plate by the kitchen door, and went back to see if he had dreamed about the cat, or if the rest of his dinner was still there. Finding the plate empty, and the

scent of the cat still lying strong, he decided to follow it.
The line took him down the garden path, through the
cabbages and potatoes, through the radish bed, among the
marrow plants, through the beans, down another lesser
gardener's path made of cinders, and so to the garden gate.
The cat had jumped the gate, but Snapper crawled under-
neath, dragging the dead chicken with him. He sniffed for
a while at a place where the cat had sat and completed its
toilet, and then followed beside a hedge until he came to
the woodstacks beyond which was the woodshed adjoining the chicken house in which the farmer had discovered
the succession of marketable corpses.

This shed was a place of much interest for Snapper. His
tail went up, his ears went up, his nose went down to the
earth, and forgetting his humiliation, he started to work
along one of the many lines of scent which were laid on the
earth. The line led him to a new hole in the corner of the
shed, into which he began to dig with great excitement.
While he was working his forepaws as fast as he could,
with pauses for deep sniffs into the earth, he heard the loud
clucking of a poult beyond the opposite wooden wall of
the shed. He heard it as he heard the lowing of cows in the
meadow waiting to be milked, as he heard the rooks in the
lime-trees, and took no heed of the clucking until additional rustlings and squeakings very near made him withdraw his head from the hole and look in their direction.

To Snapper's wildest delight he saw what hitherto he
had only seen in dreams—rats, many rats, struggling together as they dragged a chicken towards the corner where
he was standing.

In the commotion of flapping wings and squawking the
rats had not observed him until he was among them. He
nipped one lightly with his teeth and drew back quivering
from ear-tip to tail-tip as it turned at him and jibbered.
Before he could do anything one had bitten him on the
nose. Snapper leapt back in astonishment for about half a

second, then with a growl of rage he ran forward and bit the rat across the back. The rat squealed, and the noise made him shake it furiously. Meanwhile the other rats had abandoned the chicken, which was squatting on the earth spread-winged and gaping. Without pause Snapper darted after another rat, which turned on him and bared its teeth as it sat up against the wall of the shed and squealed. Snapper chopped it in his teeth, shook it as he had the other, and flung it away in order to get one more. Then from the hole in the corner, from other holes around the base of the shed, and from the faggot-stacks outside, other rats began to appear. They sat up on their hind legs and sniffed together, baring their curved yellow teeth. Snapper had disturbed the colony which only two days before had finally abandoned, owing to hunger, their assault on the new concrete floors of the granary of the hunting stables. These rats swarmed out of the holes and formed a ring around the dog, jibbering and whispering among themselves, sitting on their hindlegs and dropping again to run little distances on their fore-feet, then sitting up again. Snapper barked at them, but they did not run away. Then a big old buck rat squeaked, and Snapper ran at it. The buck rat let out a squeal, and all the rats ran to Snapper and began to swarm over him as they bit him.

It was at this moment that the farmer, having heard the cries of the pullet, and coming up in a rage from his farmyard, carrying his loaded gun in his hand, ready to shoot the dog, saw the dog in the corner beset by more than two score of rats biting his legs and his ears, hanging on to the dead chicken round his neck, while he was snarling and turning all ways to snap and bite. So astonished was the farmer that he let out a shout, and raising his gun, fired both barrels together into the rats.

When the Assistant Professor arrived at the farmyard a minute later the first thing he saw was Snapper being nursed in the arms of the farmer's wife, while the farmer

was standing among a group of neighbours, quite breath-
less as he repeated again and again what he had seen. There
were the nine rats which had been killed, three by the dog,
and six by the shot. And not one pellet, declared the
farmer, had harmed a hair of the dear little dog's head,
bless the little b'uty. But one of the lead pellets had cut the
string which attached the chicken to his neck.

The live chicken, which the rats had been dragging into
the shed, had escaped, and was sitting on the tailboard of a
cart, looking bedraggled and very subdued, but otherwise
uninjured.

9

"Yes, sir," the Professor tells successive classes of stoo-
dents, "that's Snapper, the dorg you've seen with me,
that's the dorg that ate his punishment. That's the original
Shaggy Dorg."

It happened way back in Devon, England. Snapper is
now a respectable old toothless gentleman dog, fed on
slops, inclined to be a little stiff and portly, who has his
own cushions and sets of rubber bones and invariable
ceremonies and ways of procedure inside and outside the
house. Sometimes, however, as when the moon is full, he
may go out on the campus, and dig for imaginary rats
under imaginary cypress trees, shaking them in imaginary
teeth. The Professor, after a shot or two of imaginary
Scotch, talks of his imaginary masterpiece on the French
Revolution, which one day he intends to finish. The
sophomores, or freshmen, are not particularly interested
in the projected masterpiece, however, but all of them
want to know the reason why the Professor refers in the
course of his story to "the dorg who ate his punishment".
Oh, he and Snapper went for a long walk, the Professor
tells them, and when they returned the farmer's wife came

up with a big plateful of carefully boned chicken which she had prepared for the little dog from the poults which the rats had killed.

TROUT

Motorists from London know the winding road which leads from Taunton to the sunsets of the west; up hills and round bends with valleys below, twisting and turning above wooded coombes and plunging down to cross over little bridges, through villages with ancient names, and at last to the high ridge between beechen hedges where the sombre line of the moor can be seen to the north.

As this road upon the ridge begins to descend, the observant motorist may discern, in the mists and wooded prospects below him, a distant church tower, in the shape of an owl; and here is the town of South Dulton.

The main road to London—one hundred and eighty miles eastward—runs through South Dulton. The motorist rolls through its square, and away to the western sea-board, with visions of sand and green combers, of Devonshire cream and pleasant nights in the local inns. He is gone, followed by others; the wheels roll westward, away from the town. Few stop there. It is said by the superficial that nothing ever happens in South Dulton: that its golden age departed with the stage coach and the jingle of harness. Maybe this is so; but before we, too, pass on, let us for a moment think about Mrs. Houghton-Hawton (of Hawton) before she is forgotten.

The new generation remembers its own events. Who will forget, while they live, the great event of the roasting of the ox, in the market-place, and in summer, too, during the Forces Welcome Home reception? Six hundred people attended, most of them taking but the briefest glance at what was considered to be a gruesome sight—the great coal-fire in a brick open-sided box, and the monstrous horned and staring-eyed carcass frizzling on a horizontal bar of iron. The free beer cheered things up a bit, when they sat down to trestle-tables set out in rows and ate slices of the ox with potatoes and boiled cabbage.

Lest the above be interpreted as a criticism of the Town Council's lack of imagination, let it be said at once that South Dulton, in one respect, is in the van of modernity and progress. It possesses that which exists elsewhere only in the dreams of fly-fishermen of modest means—for South Dulton, having acquired the land adjoining half a mile of the main river into which the Hawton brook flowed, then decided that the fishing rights should belong to everybody. Free salmon, sea-trout, and brown trout fishing for all comers. God made the fishes for man and here men, uninhibited by selfish landlord or vested in-terests, take their rights.

The River Dull runs below the town. At the bottom of the hill the London road is carried by a bridge with a grey stone parapet. The bridge marks the upper limit of the free fishing. Immediately below the bridge is a high weir with a stone apron sloping too steeply for the ascent of any fish except in an almost phenomenal flood. Salmon and trout running up to spawn are forced to remain below the weir—in the water of the free fishing. And just below the weir stands the inadequate town sewage plant. After that was built, the Town Council had been able to buy the fishing rights of their half-mile at their own price.

2

Motorists passing down the London road at night slow up at the bridge, for the road bends beyond it. Occasionally one stops, attracted and puzzled by the strange flashing and dancing of lights in the valley below. Scrutiny reveals that the lights are moving apparently in the river itself. Are these the fabled lights of Will-o'-the-wisp? Surely not, for in addition to the lights are to be heard shouts, accompanied by noises of splashing and beating of the water. There may be a dull explosion, and a momentary fountain arising below. The sounds of quarrelling and the snarling of dogs are not unknown in that stretch of the town's free fishing. Here no keeper, hired by selfish capitalist, can prevent men from taking their rights; no water-bailiff, hated agent of the Board of Conservancy, dare show his face on the bank.

Dazed by the little searchlights, the salmon which has run up to spawn, its skin dark brown, its flesh infirm, its body full of milt or eggs, lies close to the bottom of the pool, while gaff or wire-noose on long ash-pole is moved nearer the tail, nearer and nearer, gaff just below the ventral fin, or noose over the dark square tail. Then jerk—out he comes! Hide'n under a vuzz-bush, midear, and keep an eye on'm, for rogues abound; there are always folk ready to steal the work of honest men.

Sometimes when many fish are lying there, gangs at night blow the pits with gelignite cartridges, killing by concussion everything living in the pool. Sometimes a couple of sportsmen will throw in a large screw-top beer-bottle filled with quicklime and a little water, and weighted so that it sinks to the bottom. The carbonic-acid gas increases until its pressure shatters the bottle; and in its rush to the surface enough gas is absorbed by the water to poison nearly every fish for scores of yards. Another method is to put an old stocking filled with chloride of lime into the stream; the first mouthful of dissolved chlorine gas passing through delicate gills—the lungs of a fish—causes twisting, leaping torture, until the fish turns on its side and floats down to where on the shallows hands await to grasp and pitch their spoil on the bank.

During days of summer, when the river is dead low and bright, small boys can be observed stalking the few tiny trout, mere fingerlings, that have come up from below. Bare-legged and intent, each with a stick to which is attached a fine brass-wire noose, the boys creep after the darting fish until they are fatigued and cowed. Noose is worked over the tail. Jerk! Put it in the pocket and go after that other one. Only four inches long, and ungrown? Yes, but if I don't have'n someone else will, so I'll have'n first. That's right, my boy. You look after yourself, no one else will.

3

A mile away, on the side of a hill, stands a house, gaunt and unpainted behind the Palladian pillars of its main entrance. Once life flowed from the Big House, as Hawton Hall was called, to all the farms around it, for many miles. Now, at night, sometimes a solitary light is to be seen in one of its windows, until nine o'clock precisely: when the light goes out, and the night is to the ghosts, which are memories.

For Hawton Hall is one of those English, or it might well be said, European houses which have had their day. Hawton awaits demolition for its valuable teak and oak and mahogany doors, its beams and rafters, the lead on its roof, the oak and pitch-pine planking of its floors and the panelling of its walls. Even its stones have a value in the post-war shortage of every kind of material in Britain. There are several eager builders waiting for the death of Mrs. Houghton-Hawton (of Hawton) and the sale by auction of that valuable repository of building materials. But the châtelaine of Hawton Hall, who has known four wars and five generations of her family, is still alive.

During the second World War Hawton Hall was occupied by many families, evacuated from the towns. The parkland—which had been sold after the first war—was a camp. Concrete roads and paths and scores of squat black huts of tarred corrugated-iron and brick, shaped like headless elephants in repose, had taken the place of the beautiful timber trees and the herd of fallow-deer. But Mrs. Houghton-Hawton (of Hawton) remained, occupying four rooms of the mansion, including the old music-room, which faced west, and the sloping land to the river.

4

Nearly every morning the old lady made her way to that room, walking by the aid of an ebony stick with an ivory handle, and looked through the wide west window. The scene had long ceased actively to distress her, for she lived almost entirely in her memories. These were by no means sad—for she had a great-grandson who was, to her, all that had been, and was to be.

Upon the piano, which had not been tuned or played for many years, stood a large silver photograph-frame. Within the frame were several photographs of young men: each was clad in tweeds; each was holding a fishing-rod in one hand, and a trout in the other.

One morning when she entered the music room Mrs. Houghton-Hawton noticed that the frame was not standing as it should have been, exactly facing the west window. The sight disturbed her, and she said aloud to the air: "Oh Matilda, pray see that the frame be replaced after polishing, exactly as before." Her voice was low; a little tired, and as she spoke she was seeing the face of her lady's maid before her; and she heard the reply, dignified and quiet: "Yes, ma'am, of course the gentlemen must always see the river." But Matilda Parker had died at the age of seventy-three, a dozen years before.

Mrs. Houghton-Hawton peered at the frame and noticed with agitation that there were fingermarks on its rim. She did not see that they were small fingermarks, as of a boy's hands; and she was moving to the wire bell-pull beside the door when she rememberd in time that there would be nobody in the servants' hall to answer it. How foolish of her! Of course, the house was now divided into five parts, four of them occupied by the young wives and families of Royal Air Force officers stationed at the airfield beyond the river and the valley, on level ground on which once had stood three of the Hawton farms. Nevertheless, she was disturbed. Could Mr. Ridd the ironmonger have called again, and taken the frame in his hands to remark on it? How had he come into the room?

As a fact, Mr. Ridd, the ironmonger of South Dulton, had last come to see Mrs. Houghton-Hawton more than thirty years before. Mr. Ridd had called at Hawton Hall shortly after the opening of the fishing season one March to express his deep sorrow at "the Captain's death, as proper a young gentleman as ever whipped water with rod and line", and then in his nervousness he had taken the photograph-frame, with its embossed coat-armour, off the piano and, after staring at it with an expression of dolour, had respectfully suggested that if at any time madam would like a few trout for her breakfast, he would be only too willing to catch them for her, just for the sport of it, if she understood his meaning. Mrs. Houghton-Hawton had entirely understood Mr. Ridd's meaning, and graciously she had thanked Mr. Ridd, saying that it was most kind of Mr. Ridd to have offered his services, but at the moment . . .

Mr. Ridd had left almost hurriedly, and gone out to his Ford van standing in the courtyard of the empty stables behind the mansion, wondering if the old girl had made arrangements to let the fishing.

Mrs. Houghton-Hawton had no intention of letting the fishing. Certainly not to Mr. Ridd! The way the fellow had handled the frame, turning it about, peering at it from various angles; and then the cunning look in his eyes as he had revealed the true purpose of his visit!

In truth, Mr. Ridd, a keen fly-fisherman, had not called for the purpose of getting some fishing for himself. When he had come into the presence of the old lady, and had seen the photographs in the frame an awful doubt had entered into him that she might think he had only pretended to sympathy that her son in the Royal Flying Corps had been killed, in order to get some trouting. Mr. Ridd's sympathy had been genuine; he had admired the tall, handsome figure of the Captain, and the fine way he could throw a dry-fly (as though he were able to know how a fish felt) with the delicacy and lightness of one of the hatching water-flies rising from the surface of the stream. And Mr. Ridd, talking it over with his wife at breakfast of bacon, egg, and sausage that morning, had almost convinced himself that by offering to supply Mrs. Houghton-Hawton's table with trout he was doing so solely as a tribute to her bereavement and loneliness.

5

On the occasion of Mr. Ridd's visit, the silver frame had contained three photographs, and the space for a fourth. The two lower photographs were of the kind known as snapshots, while the uppermost was a faded daguerreotype. Each was identical in subject and composition: a young man, a rod, and a fish.

The uppermost portrait was entirely of a past age—that is to say, it had been taken when Alethea Houghton (an heiress in her own right) had been a child. The details were nearly, but not entirely, obscure by the fadings of time. There was the figure of her father-in-law, Major Hawton, wearing a small close-fitting, small-peaked cap, with high lapels to his jacket, and tight knickerbockers and high fawn gaiters. With a magnifying glass, the beholder might just discern a face with the incipient moustaches and beard and whiskers of a youth in mid-Victorian times. He held a fourteen-foot greenheart rod in one hand, a two-pound trout in the other, a couple of fingers through one of its gills. He had been killed soon afterwards, with the Light Brigade in the Crimean War.

Below the daguerretype was an early photograph, faded and yellow, of his son, who married Alethea Houghton, thus joining two landed estates and conjoining his coat-armour with that of his heiress-bride. Following the family tradition, the youth in the Norfolk jacket holding an eleven-foot rod with a ten-ounce fish had in due course become a soldier, who, leaving wife and small son at Hawton Hall, had died of enteric fever in the South African War.

The third photograph was that of the son, taken while still a schoolboy. He wore a straw boater and a jacket of Donegal tweed, while his rod was a nine-foot length of split-cane, with which he had taken his first fish, a somewhat lean half-pounder. The first World War had taken him, and with most of his generation he had found his grave in that immense desolation of linked shell-holes stretching from North Flanders to the downland country of Artois and Picardy. But before his death as an observer in the balloon section of the Royal Flying Corps he had married a girl serving with the Red Cross, and she had had a son who had grown up never having seen, or been seen by, his father. The boy had gone to the same school which many generations of Hawtons had attended; and, like them, he had learned to fish for trout with an artificial fly. In due course a fourth photograph had been added to the three others in the frame. The fish had been a six-ounce trout, taken on a three-ounce rod of split-cane eight feet long; and likewise in due course he had found a soldier's grave far from his native land, in action with his regiment of the Royal Armoured Corps, the 17th Lancers, the Death or Glory Boys, in the desert welfare with the Afrika Korps.

After her grandson's death Mrs. Houghton-Hawton had kept his rod and tackle for his son. This was the boy who had returned on holiday from school the day before our story began with Mrs. Houghton-Hawton peering at the fingermarks on her silver frame. The boy's hands had been greasy, for the first thing he had done after returning home was to rub his enamelled and tapered silk line with a piece of wash-leather on which was some paraffin-wax, in order to make the line float when he went fishing on the morrow.

Somewhat nervously the boy had surveyed the blank space in the family picture record, and wondered if he would be there with his first trout, and if it would be the biggest of them all, before the Easter holidays were over.

6

The declining weights and conditions of those fish in the photographs might have suggested to a philosophical ichthyologist a parallel in decline of the human scene and substance at Hawton Hall. For the same changes in human values had affected both land and river equally. These changes had been accepted by nearly everyone as the changes due to modern progress.

Soon after the death of the husband of Alethea Hawton the road running through the valley above the stream had been metalled and tarred for the new motor traffic which was gradually replacing the horse and the iron-shod wooden wheel. From off the sealed surfaces, laid to keep down dust, rainwater drained quickly into the river, causing it to rise and fall swiftly, and so to scour the gravelbeds which were the homes of the creepers and nymphs on which the trout fed. In addition to this disturbance, deadly tar-acids poisoned the microscopic life—the daphnia and plankton, on which the new-hatched trout fry fed.

After some years, and much endeavour to remedy injustice, deadly tar was replaced by harmless bitumen as a stone-binding surface; but by then increased drainage had caused other pollution. The fish found little on which to feed, for the gravelly bottom was silted, and most of the nymphs and other delicate water-life that can exist only in pure water had vanished. Lacking natural food, the bigger fish became cannibals, before slow starvation came upon them. A few were to be seen day after day in the same places, growing leaner and blacker, until they disappeared; only the occasional ring of a small rising fish broke the smooth flow of the water in the clear light of morning and the mellow dusk of a mid-summer evening. No mayflies arose and danced over the pools, no dark sedgeflies sped and whirled over the runs at night. The silt absorbed oxygen faster than the stream could replace it from the air in bubbles broken by every fall and run and jabble and stony shallow.

In vain the unhappy owner took legal action, pleading that the chronic pollution contravened the Rivers Pollution Act and the Public Health Acts. In vain samples of river-water were taken, in the presence of witnesses, and put into bottles which were then sealed, before being analysed and chemists' reports offered as evidence in courts of law. Technically pollution in some cases was proved, but no damages were awarded. The pollution continued as before; it was cheaper for the offending factories to face further summonses for pollution than to spend money to install filter beds and tanks.

With the building of more houses the pollution increased; but the owner did not lose heart. Little dams of tree-trunks were made, in the hope that high-water winter spates would cause turbulence to sweep away the deadly silt. In spring new water-plants were introduced, in the hope that while growing in sunlight they might absorb the noxious carbon dioxide gas, and release the oxygen which was the life of the stream, by which all things breathed. More trout were turned into the water.

The Hawton estate, once of flourishing farms held by a sturdy tenantry maintaining the fertility of the soil and looking to the squire for leadership in all things, had likewise declined. Agricultural depression, caused by importation of cheap foreign food, had been interrupted by wars which at base were trade wars. Every death in the family succession meant that a large sum had to be found to pay the death-duties to a government which was composed almost exclusively of those serving and served by the trading interests. Death-duties could be met only by the sale of farm-lands.

When all the land had of necessity been sold off, only the park and mansion remained. Further taxation caused the park and its splendid timber to be sold. A syndicate of speculators interested only in making money bought the park and sold the trees to a timber-merchant, who forthwith felled them and dragged the trunks away. A milk-canning factory was built where the old grist-mill had stood by the stream; its effluents finally killed the last of the weary trout. A gas-works did the rest. Birds forsook the banks; the last kingfisher flashed across the bends in the meadow, the last heron flapped away from water which even eels had left.

Rows of box-like houses, built of concrete, with asbestos roofs, grew where once fallow-deer had grazed. Modernity had come right up to the walls of the Hall.

A fence of galvanized wire set with concrete posts, and a macrocarpa hedge growing rapidly, as though with wild desire to hide with its greenery the change without, enclosed the unpainted mansion and its four acres of gardens, which were too costly to keep up. Slowly a wilderness of weeds arose there, until the Council rented the gardens for a nominal sum as allotments for whomsoever in South Dulton wanted an allotment. That was in the 'thirties, when the money value of English land was lower than it had been for nearly two centuries.

7

The better to inspect the photographs every morning, Mrs. Houghton-Hawton polished the lenses of her spectacles on a piece of silk which had lived in its special ivory box on the chimney-piece of the music-room for nearly thirty years. The constant friction against glass, gentle though it had been, had so worn the silk, that it looked as if it were begetting its life anew from the silkworm. In her care of that piece of silk, in her fidelity to it, might be seen the source of the old woman's fortitude to conserve what was left, after the ruin of another war, for her great-grandson.

The fragment of silk had been part of a white shining strength that swung a man slowly to earth, below the observation balloon from which he had jumped at a telephone-message of "Hun Over!" from the group frenziedly winding in the hauling-gear below; and having jumped and tugged at the release-cord, he had been pulled up with a jerk and flung about, knowing while he swung upon the wild beats of his heart that he was safe. The wind was taking him away from the slanting cable of the balloon. His fellow-observer had jumped after him, and was two hundred feet above, between himself and the balloon. Then the skirl and crack of shrapnel was joined by the hiss and clack of machine-gun bullets from above and below. He watched the vague smoky line of tracers passing diagonally by the balloon, surely through it: and yes, there was a slow curl of flame from its top. Then he saw the Hun, an Albatross, make an Immelmann turn, only to dive away to hedge-hop back to Hunland; and looking up, he saw two Sopwith Camels following the Hun down, and shooting at him. The bullets passed near; the *claquement* made his ears ring and sing, until a sudden terrific shock made him feel himself to be very far away, as he swung gently under the parachute, so gently that the sensation of swinging changed to one of gliding, then to a rippling as of the surface of a river.

As he listened, he could hear under the gentle noises of the stream on the gravelly shallows, the singing of the water-ouzel. He saw the little sturdy black and white bird perching on a mossy stone at the tail of the pool where the water ran clear and fast. He saw his father beside him, and felt the excitement of tying a dry-fly for the first time. He saw the spinners of the live duns rising and falling over the stream in the June evening. He saw the females descending to drop the eggs from the long whisks into the water. He heard the sipsucking noises of trout invisible in the fast runs, as imperceptibly they thrust up their nebs while sucking in the spent flies. He saw himself crouching beside his father on the edge of the gravel under the bank, and heard his reassuring "You'll get him, take your time, be easy." He felt clumsy. The fly would catch in the alders in front, or in the thistles on the meadow behind. He was nervous because Father was there, and as in a dream he drew out line while working the rod to and fro until the tiny hackled fly was passing overhead, and as he measured the distance to the rising trout with his eye, he felt himself suddenly to be his father, and then he was casting exactly as Father did. He shot his line and tapered cast and brown hackled fly out straight and light; the fly dropped almost dreamily on the quiet bubble-riding water beside the mossy stone where the trout lay. The fly fell lightly, and rode down beside a bubble; the neb of a fish arose and quietly sucked in the fly; a light jerk of his wrist, and the tiny hook was driven into the corner of the trout's mouth. The fish dashed downstream, the rod bent, the fish leapt shaking its head, and he saw the red spots on its golden-brown length. Careful lest it break away, for the last two links of the cast were single horsehair!

He played the trout for at least five minutes, before it turned on its side, dead-beat. His first fish! Quick, the spring-balance, before it lost weight by drying! Father had never got a trout of more than eight ounces that season! It looked so beautiful, he wanted to put it back into the river; but when it flapped nearer the edge of the grassy bank he grabbed it in alarm. As he was working the hook from the bony mouth, the hook suddenly grew very big and fixed itself in his own mouth, attached to a monstrous line which tore at his jaw. He cried out for Father, but Father was gone. He could not find Father. He cried out: "Mother!" for the river was roaring. It was swelling and turning red. The line dragged violently at his head—so terribly violently that he was dragged farther and farther from himself, until at last something snapped, and after that everything was dim and unsubstantial, and fading into vacancy.

From below they watched the cable whipping and coiling on the ground, dragging down in a smoking tangle of rope and wicker basket the body of the observer and his torn parachute. Later they sent to his mother, together with his personal belongings, a piece of the silk, and a photograph of his grave at Ervillers.

That had been in 1917. Since then there had been another grave, in the desert of North Africa. But there was also another Nigel, just home from school for the Easter holidays, and eager to catch his first fish. All the eldest Hawton sons, back to the Tudors and beyond, had borne the name of Nigel.

But where could Nigel fish? Grannie had been worrying about it; and in the end had remembered Mr. Jones, who once had mentioned something about the free fishing below the London road.

8

Mr. Jones was known as a taxi-driver. This was a misnomer in some respect, for Mr. Jones's motorcar was not fitted with a taximeter, and it was, moreover, a Rolls-

Royce, licensed to carry six passengers, certainly, but—well, no more need be said, except that the Silver Ghost chassis dated from 1914, and that its first owner had been the châtelaine of Hawton Hall.

The present owner-driver of the elderly motorcar was by name Jones; but he was prepared to resent anyone calling him by that name, especially any old die-hard Tory. Most of his fares called him either nothing, or Mr. Jones, or Charley; but Jones, he wouldn't have any of that, especially from any old geezer who never spent more than a couple of quid a year with him!

To the South Dulton free-fishing went Mrs. Hawton and her great-grandson Nigel on the second day of the Easter holidays. They arrived in Mr. Jones's motor. After the rather long business of the old lady removing herself, with the aid of her ebony walking-stick, from the back of the landau, the two began to move towards the bank. Mr. Jones walked behind them, carrying, at Mrs. Hawton's request, the tea-basket, Mr. Nigel's rod, and a landing net.

Mr. Jones (who was not, it need hardly be said, a native of South Dulton, but a comparatively recent immigrant) thought, as he puffed at his fag, that he didn't mind carrying the rod to oblige the dame, but, as far as he was concerned, he wasn't going to Mister no blooming boy, or man either for that matter.

The party of three stopped by the river-bank. The water ran clear over stones with sandy scours at the eddies, for the outfall of the sewage plant was below, hidden by trees. Unspeaking, with a faint smile, the driver handed the hollow bamboo rod-case to the boy.

"I say, Gran, this *is* the Palakoma split-cane that Daddy killed his first fish with, isn't it? It's wizard! Look, it's a hexagon pattern, Mr. Jones! They're awfully hard to get now. Bayley-Martin at school says it's the best rod for small streams in the world!"

Pleased with the way he had been addressed, Mr. Jones watched the eager fingers attaching the reel, and drawing

out line to pass it through the rings. Despite the rubbing
with paraffin-wax and wash-leather, the line was tacky
with age, and seemed reluctant to leave the spool.

"Now I believe I ought to have kept it on the line-drier!"
the old lady remarked, watching the boy's actions intently
through her lorgnette. "I recollect your grandfather always kept his lines between the page of a copy of *The
Times* every year, until the season opened again. I do hope
you will find the flies of use, my dear. I don't suppose the
change of fashion in flies is so marked as in other things."
Her voice quavered a little; she was lost awhile; but recovered herself, and saw the boy before her once
again.

The boy and the man were examining the several var-
iegated objects in their little compartments, each with its
minute hinged mica lid that flipped open at a touch.

"Now I wonder which flies you should use?" the frail
voice enquired, with careful distinctiveness of tone.
"Your grandfather was always saying something about
wet-flies. Now what is the difference, I wonder?"

"Bayley-Martin always swears by the dry-fly, Gran. He
says he's a dry-fly purist, and would never think of fishing
wet."

As a fact, the fourteen-year-old boy referred to as a
dry-fly purist had never caught any fish bigger than a
salmon-parr, that voracious six-inch snap-all-that-floats-
and-swims fish looking like a trout but with dark fin-
gerprints on its side; and his fishing had been confined to the
moorland stream of his Cumberland home; but Bayley-
Martin was a great reader, and lived mainly in the
imagination.

"A pity Bayley-Martin isn't here," observed Mr. Jones.
"Myself, I'm a worm poorist. None of this whipping
water for me. When the river's in flood, and muddy, that's
the time to yank 'em out."

"Don't you think that as at the moment the water has
the appearance of what used to be described as gin-clear,"

remarked the old lady, "it might be as well to try a dry-fly?"

"Well, others may be a better judge o' gin than what I be," retorted the driver, looking up at the sky, and wishing that his pals in the Ring of Bells could hear him.

"Now will you please be so good as to tell Mr. Nigel which are the dry-flies, and which are the wet, Mr. Jones?"

Mr. Jones was so relieved at the obvious respect shown to himself that he replied earnestly: "I'm sorry I don't know, ma'am. But mebbe one's so good as another. To tell you the honest truth, ma'am, I've watched them as knows putting on a fly and taking it off again, and trying others, and when they weren't no good, whipping 'em off again and picking out another, quizzing it, and putting it back sticking it into their hat until they look like a fly-paper. Never satisfied, is a fly-fisherman. I don't wonder, either, when you come to think of it. All these colours ain't natural. Look at this one—" He dropped a minute and delicate affair of red and green peacock-feather, silk, varnish, and steel into his palm and held it out. "What fish is going to recognize that as anything he's seen before? And this—what natural fly, in a manner o' speaking, has two white wings and a lot of ginger whiskers growing out of its body?" He turned to the boy. "See? I ask you! But a worm's a worm all the world over, and the natural food of a fish, if you see my meaning."

Nigel, conscious of his school motto *Manners makyth man,* smiled pleasantly. But he thought: A wormer! "I wonder if this fly is meant to represent a worm?" he asked, picking up an object of fluffy cinnamon with a double hook.

Mr. Jones gave it a glance, and said emphatically: "Naow! That's an eel fly, for the eel has a double lock to its jaws, and can wriggle out o' one hook, but never two."

Nigel thought this an odd explanation, for according to the coloured plates in his book it was a Scottish loch-fly for big trout.

"I should try this one, if I were you," advised Mr. Jones, picking up a mayfly. "It's a juicy mouthful." As he spoke the stub of a cigarette was wagging about on his lower lip.

"Yes, Nigel," said Mrs. Houghton-Hawton, "I am sure that Mr. Jones is right about the choice of fly being not of the greatest importance. Your grandfather used to say, I remember, that to fish with a fly you believe in, is nine-tenths of the way to persuading a fish to believe in it also."

"How about this red and green joker?" asked Mr. Jones. "Here, give us the gut."

"I say, thank you so much, but I can tie it on," assured the boy, struggling to conceal his anxiety. "I know the turle knot—Bayley-Martin swears that's the best."

"I've nearly done it now," said the driver.

"Thank you," replied Nigel, politely, while his lip trembled.

"There you are, my lad," exclaimed Mr. Jones, flipping the fly away on the gut leader with his finger and thumb. At the same time he loosened the cigarette from his lower lip and neatly using an expulsion of air compressed within his cheeks flipped the stub into the river. At that moment a salmon rolled up to the top of the pool, showed a yellow-grey blue as it turned, and went under again. "There, did you see that, Nigel?" he cried, pointing to the water. "A bloomin' great fish come up and nosed it! Quick, chuck your fly in the same place!"

"I saw it, Gran, a salmon!" cried the boy. He dropped the flybox in his excitement, and went on his hands and knees to seek the flies which had shot out of some of the compartments. "Oh, curse, just my luck."

"Here, try this white-winged thing," suggested Mr. Jones. "After all, my fag-end was white."

"Yes, why not take Mr. Jones's advice, Nigel? The rise may be over at any moment. I remember your grandfather used to say a rise might begin suddenly, and end as suddenly."

"Some water-whippers use several flies at once," said

the driver, when he had tied the red-and-green Alexandra to the end of the cast. "That's your tail-fly. I'll tie white-wings above it." He snapped a length of gut from the cast. "That's all right, don't worry. It'll tie again. Have it hanging like this, see, on a bit by itself. That's called a dropper. One more on top, any one'll do, that's your tickler. Here, you tie it, and I'll find a worm to shove on fur luck." He began kicking up the turf, ceasing as another man came through the gate at the top of the slope, carrying a rod-case in one hand and a net in the other.

"Ah, here's Mr. Ridd," cried Mrs. Houghton-Hawton. "He'll be able to tell us what is the best fly to use, I have no doubt."

Jones abruptly ceased his prospecting for worms, and standing up, stretched his arm, pushed back his driver's cap, yawned, and sought a cigarette. Another old-fashioned codger!

9

Mr. Ridd's respectful pleasure in meeting Mrs. Houghton-Hawton and Master Nigel at the river was genuine. Any eager mental pictures he had had of getting a salmon with his new American stainless steel three-foot rod, using a small bronze Devon spinner on a threadline of gut-substitute with a Pffleuger spinning-reel, were put aside. This new outfit, given him by an American officer after a day's fishing together, was capable of throwing a minnow weighing an ounce for great distances, and of dropping it within a foot of where he wanted to drop it. With such a rod and reel the American expert had cast well up-river, and worked the minnow downstream in a deadly manner, which had taken several sea-trout and a salmon in one afternoon, while Mr. Ridd had caught nothing. He had received the outfit by post that morning as a parting gift from the American officer, who was going back to the States. All the morning Mr. Ridd had been awaiting one o'clock, for it was the day of South Dulton's early-closing; but now, seeing Mrs. Houghton-Hawton by the riverside, and apprehending her gracious request for advice, Mr. Ridd forgot his ambition in a desire to be of service.

Immediately he declared that the red-and-green silver-bodied Alexandra was no good. It might be all right in Blagdon reservoir near Bristol, but it was useless in the present water. The Coachman was no good, either. All right for the late evening, with its white wings, but not a bit of use during the day. As for the bob-fly goodness gracious, wherever did it come from? A proper Irish sea-trout lough lure—a Parson Hughes it looked like, or it might be a Fiery Forbes, or even a local variation of Grouse and Claret. Off it came. What he would recommend was one or another of the Pale Wateries.

Finally Mr. Ridd selected a Blue Upright, a Cow Dung, and a Coch-y-Bondhu, which he pronounced Cocky Bundy, for the bobfly. A Cocky Bundy, he explained, was a Welsh beetle found near bracken, and was a killing fly all the year. You couldn't beat a Cocky Bundy.

"I bet it don't beat a worm," remarked Mr. Jones.

"Mr. Jones has a single-minded faith in worms," said the old lady, and Mr. Ridd nodded politely in agreement. He, too, fished the worm in coloured water; it was catch-as-catch-can on the Free Fishing.

The flies having been tied, Mr. Ridd suggested that Master Nigel should kneel on the bank, lest the fish see him or the flash of his rod. Would madam kindly step back with him and Mr. Jones?

They retired, and the boy, praying that his nervousness would not be noticed, began to cast. He waved his arm from the shoulder, forgetting the instructions of Bayley-Martin.

"Keep that elbow well into your side, sir!" cried Mr.

Ridd. "You'll excuse me telling of him, ma'am? Imagine you're holding a whisky bottle under your arm, and use the wrist only, with the spring of the rod." Then, an awful thought of what he had said occurring to him, he turned to Mrs. Houghton-Hawton, stammering: "No particular reference intended, ma'am, about the whisky bottle. Really, ma'am, it's just the usual advice to the tyro, if you understand my meaning, ma'am."

"I think Mr. Nigel will understand, Mr. Ridd. He comes of a family of fly-fishermen."

"Of course, ma'am. And if you'll pardon the remark, ma'am, but I sincerely hope that the photograph of his first trout will be took this very day."

Just as he had spoken, the boy leapt up: he struck violently in his excitement; there was a glint in the air with the backward flinging of the line: a small fish leaping on the grass.

"A proper trout," was Mr. Ridd's verdict. "Three ounces, a sizeable fish. Well over the seven-inch limit."

The boy's hand trembled as he worked the hook from the prickly tongue, afterwards breaking the fish's neck. "Oh, Gran, aren't the red spots lovely? I say, I'm a fool to have struck so hard, but it was so unexpected. I'll leave it here with you. I mustn't lose any time, now the rise is on, must I? I say, if only Bayley-Martin were here!"

During the rest of the afternoon Mr. Jones resigned himself to the incurable obstinacy of some people who wouldn't learn that a worm was the natural food of a trout. A fluke, that solitary sprat of Nigel's. Old Ridd got nothing, neither, for all his talk of invisible line and minnows coming downstream so fast that no trout could resist having a bash at it. Call that fishing? Whipping water, that's what it was, he thought, as he drove them home in the high-bodied 1914 Rolls-Royce landau which once had belonged to Hawton Hall.

10

Having helped Gran from the car, Nigel rushed away on a
most important mission. In the kitchen he explained to
Mrs. Bowden that the fish must be cooked for Gran's
dinner. Cook said that she would fry it in olive-oil before
the plaice, and she would serve it with a slip of lemon—
that was the way the Captain best liked a trout done.
"Leave it to me, dearie, I'll make it—hullo, there's her
royal highness calling me." Mrs. Bowden shuffled away,
to return a short while afterwards, saying that she wasn't
sure if there was such a thing as a bottle of beer in the
pantry.

In the hall stood Mr. Jones, cap in hand, fag-end pinched
out and stuck behind his ear, and an expression of anxious
friendliness on his face, as he listened to Mrs. Houghton-
Hawton saying to the boy: "You'd like to ask Mr. Jones to
have some beer, wouldn't you, darling? He was a most
helpful ghillie, wasn't he? I'm sure his selection of flies
would have been as suitable as any other selection. Thank
you, Bowden, may we have it on the table? Please help
yourself, Mr. Jones."

While Mr. Jones was absorbing the gassy bottled beer as
swiftly as he could in order to get away, Grannie called
Nigel into the library, and behind the door entirely con-
cealed by rows of dummy books bound in calf she put
half-a-crown into his hand. "One should tip one's ghillie,
don't you think, darling? When he goes. I won't look, then
he will think it's your own idea. Just say, 'Jones, thank you
for your help'. Perhaps if you called him Mr. Jones he
might be offended. Ghillies are most particular about such
things, dear."

"Yes, Gran," said Nigel.

The old lady had the satisfaction of observing her grandson performing this rite, and of hearing the words:
"Thank you, I'm sure, Master Nigel, sir."

Grannie produced the line-drier, and the boy carefully wound the sticky, ruined line upon it. Afterwards he went to his bedroom to examine a shelf of books that had been saved specially for him when the library had been sold to help pay death-duties when his father had been killed in 1941. He was reading a little book called *The Art of Trout Fishing on Rapid Streams; comprising a Complete System of Fishing in North Devon Streams, and their Like: with detailed instructions in the Art of Fishing with the Artificial Fly, the Natural Fly, the Fern Web, Beetle, Maggot, Worm, and Minnow, both Natural and Artificial,* when the dressing gong sounded. As he went upstairs to put on his dark-blue suit he remembered something suddenly; and the thought struck through him with almost a physical blow. He ran down the stairs shouting: "Oh, Grannie, Grannie, we forgot to take the photograph! Grannie, the photograph! Quick, quick!"

He leapt down the last flight of stairs two and three at a time, lost count in his agitation, fell over the last four steps, picked himself up in desperate haste on the tessellated white-and-black floor of the hall, and dashed down a corridor into the kitchen. Even his haste did not prevent him pausing a moment to knock on the door before opening it. "Oh, Mrs. Bowden! Quick! The photograph! Where's my trout, quick! Oh, it's cooked, it's cooked," he cried, and ran out of the kitchen again. Biting his lip against the tears that would not be stopped, he hid himself in a dark corner for a moment. Then, hearing Grannie's voice calling him, he went to find her, trying hard to smile and to suppress his sobs.

"But, darling, it isn't too late to take a photograph—there's still a little sunshine left," said Grannie in her tremulous tones, as she stroked his head. "And think how original a photograph it will be, with you holding your first trout, all ready cooked on a plate! I don't suppose Bayley-Martin has thought of that. Now put your rod together, and Bowden, who has a very steady hand, shall take the photograph, just where the others were taken. Perhaps two photographs, in case one goes wrong."

So it was done, and everything was happy again.

11

Visitors to Hawton Hall now see the photographs of five generations of fly-fishermen in the big silver frame on the piano in the music-room; and when they ask about Nigel Hawton, they are told that he is in New Zealand, where he is working on a farm, and where the trout, he writes, are simply monsters, the finest in the world. Mrs. Houghton-Hawton (of Hawton), who will be a hundred years old next year, is living for the moment when she will see again the son of her dear boy's son, and perhaps *his* little boy; and then she is lost in memories centred on the photographs in the silver frame which faces the river, and the sunset which she awaits with trust and serenity.

THE HELLER

In March the high spring-tides lap with their ragged and undulating riband of flotsam the grasses near the top of the sea-wall; and once in a score of years the south-west gales piles the sea in the estuary so high that it lops over the bank and rushes down to the reclaimed grazing marsh within. The land-locked water returns on the ebb by way of the reedy dykes, through the culverts under the wall with their one-way hinged wooden doors, and by muddy channels to the sea again.

I was unfortunate enough to miss seeing such a flood following the Great Gale, when many big trees, most of them elms but not a few beech and oak, went down; but hearing of it, I went down to the marsh the next afternoon before the time of high tide, hoping to see the water brimming over again. I wandered along the sea-wall, where the hoof-holed path of clay still held sea-water, as far as the black hospital ship *Nyphen,* and then I returned. The gale had blown itself out, a blue sky lay beyond Hartland Point, far out over the calm Atlantic.

There is a slanting path leading to the road below by the marshman's cottage, and by this I left the wide prospect seen from the sea-wall. While descending I noticed that the grasses down the inner slope were washed flat and straggly by the heavy overflooding of the day before.

The marshman was standing in the porch of the cottage, looking at his ducklings which had hatched about a fortnight since. He wore his spectacles and had a book in his hands. We greeted each other, and I stopped to talk.

I always enjoyed talking with the marshman. His face pleased me. I liked his kind brown eyes, his grey hair, his small and intelligent sea-brown face. His dog had recently been kicked by a bullock, and had a broken leg which the marshman had set with a wooden splint. This knocked on the ground as the dog trotted about with apparent ease. The marshman was a skilful man: I remembered how he had saved the life of a sheep the year before, when it was staggering crazily, because, said the marshman, it had a worm in its brain. The marshman had held the sheep's head between his knees, cut a hole in its skull with a knife, and drawn out the tapeworm by suction through a quill cut from the pinion feather of a goose. It was an even chance, for most sheep so afflicted have to be destroyed. This ewe got well, and—but the story is about the mysterious loss of the marshman's ducklings, not of mutton.

In a soft voice he began telling me about the book in his hands, which he said was "wonderful and most interesting". It was thick, and heavy, and printed in small, close-set type. It was *The History of the Jews,* and the marshman had been reading it with the same care and patience with which, year after year, he had cut the reeds in the dykes, and scythed the thistles in the rank grass. For years he had been reading that book, and he had not yet reached the middle pages.

Would I like to take the book home with me and have a read of it? He was a bit busy just now and could easily spare it for a day or two. I was quite welcome to take it, if . . .

2

I was saved from a reply by the sudden change in the marshman's face. He was staring intently beyond the gate by which we stood. His spectacles were pushed back from his eyes. I looked in the direction of his stare, and saw the usual scene—fowls on the stony and feathery road, and a couple of pigs nosing among them; the downhanging branches of the willow tree over the dyke; the green pointed leaves of the flag-iris rising thickly along both banks; the sky-gleams between them. On the water a brood of yellowish-white ducklings were paddling, watched anxiously from the road by the hen that had hatched them.

"The heller!"

At the muttered angry words the marshman's dog, which had assumed a stiff attitude from the moment of his master's fixed interest in something as yet unsmelled, unseen, and unheard by itself, whined and crouched and sprang over the gate. It had gone a few yards, sending the hens clucking and flying in all directions, when the marshman shouted. Seeing its master's arm flung to the left, the dog promptly turned in that direction. I saw its hackles rise. The narrow dyke, which brought fresh drinking water to the grazing marsh, was crossed under the willow tree by a clammer, or single heavy plank of elm-wood. As the dog ran on to the clammer I saw something at the farther end slide into the water. I had a fleeting impression of the vanishing hindquarters of a squat and slender dog, dark brown as a bulrush, and with the palms of its feet widely webbed as a duck's. It had a long tail, tapering to a point. The brown tail slid over the plank flatly yet swiftly, and disappeared without splash into the slight ripple made by the submerging animal.

"'Tis that darned old mousy-coloured fitch," grumbled the marshman opening the gate. "It be after my ducklings. It took one just about this time yesterday. Yurr, Ship!"—to the dog. "Fetch un, Ship!" The dog sprang around barking raucously, and trotted along the plank again, nose between paws, and whining with excitement where the otter had stood. Then it looked at its master and barked at the water.

While it was barking the ducklings, about fifteen yards away, began to run on the water, beating their little flukey stumps of wings and stretching out their necks. *Queep!*

Queep! Queep! they cried. The foster-hen on the bank was clucking and jerking her comb about in agitation.

"Ah, you heller, you!" cried the marshman, as a duckling was drawn under by invisible jaws. The other ducklings waddled out by the brimming edge of the road, and made for the hen in two files of uniform and tiny yellowish bodies aslant with staining to reach the cover of wings. Very red and jerky about the comb and cheekpendules, with flickering eyes, this motherly fowl squatted on the stones and lowered her wings till they rested on her useless pinion shafts, and fluffed out her feathers to make room for the eight mites which, in spite of her constant calls and entreaties, would persist in walking on that cold and unwalkable place, which was only for sipping-from at the edge.

Peep peep peep, quip pip queep weep, whistled the ducklings drowsily, in their sweet and feeble voices.

The marshman came out of the cottage with a gun.

"The heller!" he said. "The withering beast, it ought to be kicked to flames!"

He waited five minutes, watching the water where the duckling had gone down.

Parallel lines of ripples, wavering with infirm and milk-white sky, rode along the brimming water. The tide was still rising. Twenty yards away the young strong leaves of the flag-irises began to quiver. We waited. The *peep-peeps* of the happy ducklings ceased.

Water began to run, in sudden starts, around the smoothed stones in the roadway. The tide was rising fast. A feather was carried twirling on a runnel that stopped by my left toe; and after a pause it ran on a few inches, leaving dry specks of dust and a bud-sheaths tacked to the welt.

The outline of the dyke was lost in the overbrimming of the water. Grasses began to float and stray at its edges. The runnels curiously explored the least hollow; running forward, pausing, turning sideways or backwards, and blending, as though gladly, with one another.

3

"It be gone," said the marshman, lowering the gun, to my relief, for its double barrels had been near my cheek, and they were rusty, thin as an egg-shell at the muzzle, and loaded with an assortment of broken screw-heads, nuts, and odd bits of iron. He was as economical with his shooting as he was with his reading. Originally the gun had been a flintlock, owned by his great-grandfather; and his father had had it converted into a percussion cap. Its walnut stock was riddled with worm-holes; and even as I was examining it, I heard the sound like the ticking of a watch, which ceased after nine ticks. The deathwatch beetle. It was doubtful which would go first—the stock "falling abroad" in its tunnelled brittleness, or the barrels bursting from frail old-age.

"It's a high spring tide," I said, stepping farther back. "I suppose the otter came up on it, and down the dyke?"

Then the marshman told me about the 'heller'. We stood with our backs to the deep and ancient thorn hedge that borders the road to the east, a hedge double-sheared by wind and man, six feet high and eight feet thick and so matted that a man could walk along it without his boots sinking. It was grey and gold with lichens. I had always admired the hedge by the marsh toll-gate. I leaned gingerly against it while the marshman told me that he had seen the otter on the two afternoons previously, and both times when the tide was nearly on the top of the flood. No, it did not come up the dyke; it was a bold beast, and came over the sea-wall, where the tide had poured over two afternoons ago. "My wife zeed'n running over the wall, like a little brown dog. I reckon myself th' heller comes from the duckponds over in Heanton marsh, and sleeps by day in th' daggers, or goin' on up to the pillhead, and over the basin of the weir into fresh water, after trout. Never before have I heard tell of an otter going time after time, and by day, too, after the same ducklings."

I was listening intently. Was that a low, flute-like whistle . . .?

" 'Tis most unusual, zur, for an artter will always take fish when he can get fish, eels particularly, and there be plenty of eels all over the marsh. An artter loveth an eel; 'tis its most natural food, in a manner of speaking. 'Tis what is called an ambulance baste, the artter be, yes 'tis like a crab, that can live in both land and water, a proper ambulance baste it be. A most interestin' baste, for those that possess th' education vor to study up all that sort of thing. Now can 'ee tell me how an artter serves an eel different from another fish? Other fish, leastways those I've zin with my own eyes, are ate head downwards; but an eel be ate tail virst, and the head and shoulders be left. I've a' zin scores of eels, and all ate tail virst!"

While the old fellow was speaking, the water in irregular pourings and innocent swirls was stealing right across the road. It reached the hen, who, to judge from the downward pose of her head, regarded it as a nuisance A runnel slipped stealthily between her cane-coloured feet, wetting the claws worn with faithful scratching for the young. She arose, and strutted away in the lee of the hedge, calling her brood; and *Wock! Wock! Wet!* she cried, for with tiny notes of glee the ducklings had headed straight for the wide water gleaming with the early sunset.

The marshman said, "Darn the flood!" for *The History of the Jews,* container of future years' laborious pleasure, lay in a plash by the gate ten strides away. He picked it up, regarding ruefully the dripping cover. He was saying that it wasn't no odds, a bit of damp on the outside, when I noticed a small travelling ripple in the shape of an arrow moving out from the plank now almost awash. It continued steadily for about three yards from the plank, and then the arrow-head ceased to push. Ripples spread out slowly, and beyond the ripples a line of bubbles like shot began to rise and lie still. The line, increasing steadily by lengths varying from two or three to a dozen inches, drew out towards the ducklings.

I took long strides forward beside the marshman. Our footfalls splashed in the shallow water. The dog trotted at his heels, quivering, its ears cocked. A swirl arose in the leat and rocked the ducklings; they cried and struck out for the grass, but one stayed still, trying to rise on weeny wings, and then it went under.

"The *heller*!" cried the marshman, raising his gun.

For about twenty seconds we waited.

A brown whiskered head, flat and seal-like, with short rough hairs and beady black eyes, looked out of the water. *Bang!* It dived at the flash, and although we peered and waited for at least a minute after the whining of a screw-head ricocheting away over the marsh had ceased, I saw only our spectral faces shaking the water.

4

The next afternoon I went down by the eastern sea-wall, and lay on the flat grassy ridge, with a view of the lower end of the Ram's-horn duckpond. Wildfowl were flying round the marsh and settling on the open water hidden between thick green reeds. Many scores had their nests in the preserve. Why did the otter, I wondered, come all the way to the dyke when it could take all the ducklings it wanted in the pond? Perhaps in my reasoning I was falling into the old error of ascribing to a wild beast something of human reasoning; for had I been an otter after ducklings I should certainly have stayed where they were most numerous.

The tide flowed past me, with its usual straggle of froth covering the flotsam of corks, bottles, clinker, spruce-bark from the Bideford shipyards, tins, cabbage leaves, and sticks. Two ketches rode up on the flood, the exhausts

of their oil engines echoing with hollow thuds over mud
and water. I wondered why they were wasting oil, when
the current was so swift to carry them; but when they
made fast to their mooring buoys, and the bows swung
round, I realized the use of the engines—to keep them
head-on in the fairway. Of course! Gulls screamed as they
floated around the masts and cordage of the black craft,
awaiting the dumping overboard of garbage. I waited for
an hour, but saw nothing of the otter.

"Did ee see'n?" asked the marshman when I went back.
His gun lay on the table, and Ship the dog was crouched on
the threshold, nose on paws pointing to the clammer
bridge over the dyke.

"He's took another duckling,' growled the man.

The otter must have made an early crossing while I was
lazing on the bank. Perhaps he had come through a
culvert, squeezing past the sodden wooden trap; and then,
either seeing or winding me, had crossed under water. The
marshman, happening to come to the door, had seen the
duckling going under, and although he had waited for ten
minutes, nothing had come up.

"Ship here went nosing among the daggers, but
couldn't even get wind of'n. I reckon that ambulance baste
can lie on the bottom and go to sleep if it has a mind to."

By ambulance he meant amphibious, I imagined. An
otter has no gills; it breathes in the ordinary way, being an
animal that has learned to swim and hunt under water.

"Didn't you see even a bubble?"

"Not one!"

It seemed strange. Also, it had seemed strange that the
engines of the ketches were 'wasting' oil. That had a
perfectly ordinary explanation . . . when one realized it!

"And it took a duck in just the same way as before?"

"That's it! In a wink, that duck went down under."

"But didn't the ducklings see the otter?"

"Noomye! The poor li'l butie was took quick as a
wink." He was much upset by it.

"Now I'll tell ee what I'll do," he said. "I'll till a gin for a rat, I will, and if I trap an artter, will, 'twill be a pity, as the artter-'untin' gentry would say; but there 'tis!"

Otters were not generally trapped in the country of the Taw and Torridge rivers, as most of the riparian owners subscribed to the otter-hounds. There were occasions, however, when a gin was tilled, or set, on a submerged rock where an otter was known to touch, or on a sunken post driven into the river-bed near its holt. About once in a season the pack drew the brackish waters of the Ram's-horn Duckpond, but an otter was very rarely killed there, as there was impregnable holding among the thick reeds. I looked at the marshman's face, filled with grim thoughts about the heller (had he got the term from *The History of the Jews?*) and remembered how, only the year before, when an otter had been killed near Branton Church, he had confided to me that he didn't care much for "art-ter'untin' "; that it was "not much sport with all they girt dogs agin one small baste".

"I've got some old rabbit gins," said the marshman. "And I'll till them on the clammer, and get that heller, I will."

I went away to watch the mating flight of the golden plover over the marsh, and the sun had gone down behind the low line of the sandhills to the west, when I returned along the sea-wall. Three rabbit gins—rusty affairs of open iron teeth and flat steel springs ready to snap and hold anything that trod on them—lay on the plank. The marshman had bound lengths of twisted brass rabbitwire around the plank and through the ends of the chains, so that, dragged into the dyke, the weight of the three gins would drown any struggling otter.

5

My road home lay along the edge of the dyke, which was immediately under the sea-wall. Old upturned boats, rusty anchors, rotting bollards of tree-trunks and other gear lay on the wall and its inner grassy slope. Near the pill-head the brown ribs of a ketch, almost broken up, lay above the wall. I came to the hump where the road goes over the culvert. Leaning on the stone parapet, I watched the fresh water of the river moving with dark eddies under the fender into the dyke, and the overflow tumbling into the concrete basin of the weir and sliding down the short length to the rising tide. It barely rippled. The air was still and clear, bright with eve-star and crescent moon.

The last cart had left the Great Field, the faint cries of lambs arose under the moon, men were all home to their cottages, or playing skittles in the village inns. Resting the weight of my body on the stone, I stared vaguely at the water, thinking how many strange impulses and feelings came helter-skelter out of a man, and how easy it was to judge him falsely by any one act or word. The marshman had pitied a hunted otter; he had raged against a hunting otter; he felt tenderly and protectively towards the duck-lings; he would complacently stab their necks when the peas ripened, and sell them for as much money as he could get for them. In the future he would not think otter-hunting a cruel sport. And if the otter-hunters heard that he had trapped and drowned an otter, they would be sincerely upset that it had suffered such a cruel and, as it were, an unfair death. Perhaps the only difference between animal and man was that the animal had fewer notions . . .

I was musing in this idle manner, my thoughts slipping away as water, when I heard a sound somewhere behind me. It was a thin piercing whistle, the cry of an otter. Slowly I moved back my head, till only a part of my face would be visible in silhouette from the water below. I watched for a bubble, a sinuous shadow, an arrowy ripple, a swirl; I certainly did not expect to see a fat old dog-otter come drifting down on his back, swishing with his rudder and bringing it down with great thwacking splashes on the water while he chewed a half-pound trout held in his short paws. My breath ceased; my eyes held from blinking. I had a perfect view of his sturdy body, the yellowish-white patch of fur on his belly below his ribs, his sweeping whiskers, his dark eyes. Still chewing, he bumped head-on into the sill, kicked himself upright, walked on the concrete, and stood there crunching, while the five pools running from his legs and rudder ran into one. He did not chew, as I had read in books of otters chewing; he just stood there on his four legs, the tail-half of the trout sticking out of his mouth, and gulped down the bits. That trout disappeared in about ten seconds. Then the otter leaned down to the water and lapped as a cat does.

He was old, slow, coarse-haired, and about thirty pounds in weight—the biggest otter I had seen, with the broadest head.

After quenching his thirst he put his head and shoulders under water, holding himself from falling in by his stumpy webbed forefeet, and his rudder, eighteen inches long, pressing down straight behind. He was watching for fish. As though any fish remained in the waterflow after that dreaded apparition had come splashing under the culvert!

With the least ripple he slid into the water. I breathed and blinked with relief, but dared not move otherwise. A head looked up almost immediately, and two dark eyes stared at me. The otter sneezed, shook the water out of his small ears, and sank away under. I expected it to be my last sight of the beast, and leaning over to see if an arrowy ripple pointed upstream, I knocked a piece of loose stone off the parapet. To my amazement he came up near the sill again, with something in his mouth. He swung over on his back, and bit it in play. He climbed on to the sill and dropped it there, and slipped back into the water. It was the stone that had dropped from the parapet!

I kept still. The otter reappeared with something white in his mouth. He dropped it with a tinkle beside the stone, and the tinkle must have pleased him, for he picked up the china sherd—it looked like part of a teacup with the handle—and rolled over with it in his paws.

As in other Devon waters, the stream was a pitching place for cottage rubbish; and during the time I was standing by the parapet watching the otter at his play he had collected about a dozen objects—rusty salmon tins, bits of broken glass, sherds of clome pitchers and jamjars, and one-half of a sheep's jaw. He ranged them on the sill of the weir, tapping the more musical with a paw, as a cat does, until they fell into the water, when he would dive for and retrieve them.

6

At the end of about half an hour the sea was lapping over the top of the sill and pressing under the fender. Soon the dyke began to brim. The taste of salt-water must have made the otter hungry again, or perhaps he had been waiting for the tide, for he left his playthings and, dropping into the water, went down the dyke towards the marshman's cottage. I crept stealthily along the grassy border of the road, watching the arrowy ripple gleaming with the silver of the thin curved moon. The hillside under the ruined chapel above the village of Branton began to show yellow speckles of light in distant houses. The dyke being deserted (for the brood of ducklings with their hen had been shut up for the night) why then that sudden swirl and commotion in the water by the flag-irises, just where the ducklings had been taken before?

Bubbles broke on the water in strings—big bubbles.

Then something heaved glimmering out of the leat, flapping and splashing violently. The noises ceased, and more bubbles came up; the water rocked. Suddenly the splashing increased, and seemed to be moving up and down the leat, breaking the surface of the water. Splashes wetted my face. A considerable struggle was going on there. After a minute there was a new noise—the noise of sappy stalks of the flags being broken. Slap, slap, slap, on the water. I saw streaks and spots of phosphorescence or moon-gleams by the end of the plank. The flapping went on in the meadow beyond the flags, with a sound of biting.

I stood without moving for some minutes, while the biting and squirming went on steadily. My shoes filled with water. The water had spread silently half across the road. Then the noises ceased. I heard a dull rap, as of something striking the heavy wooden plank under water; a strange noise of blowing, a jangle of iron and a heavy splash, and many bubbles and faint knocking sounds. The otter had stepped on the plank to drink, and was trapped.

At last the marshman, having closed *The History of the Jews,* placed his spectacles in their case, drawn on his boots, put on his coat, taken his gun off the nails on the ceiling beam, put it back for a fluke-spearing pronged fork in the corner, lit the hurricane lamp, said with grim triumph, "Now us will go vor to see something!" He was highly pleased that he had outwitted the otter.

"There be no hurry, midear," he said. "Give'n plenty of time vor to see the water for the last occasion in his skin."

We stood for a while by the clammer, under the dark and softly shivering leaves of the willow looming over us in the lamplight.

The water had receded from the plank when the last feeble tug came along the brass wire.

The marshman, watched by his dog hopping round and round on its wooden leg in immense excitement, pulled up the bundle of gins, and the sagging beast held to them by a forepaw. It was quite dead; but the marshman decided to leave it there all night, to make certain.

"I see in the paper," he said, "that a chap up to Lunnon be giving good money for the best artter skins"—tapping the spearing handle significantly with his hand.

When it had been dropped in the water again we went a few paces into the meadow with the lamp, and by its light we saw a conger eel, thick through as a man's arm, lying in the grass. The dark living sinuousness was gone from it; and stooping, we saw that it had been bitten through the tail. Suddenly I thought it must have come with the high spring-tide over the seawall; and soon afterwards, the keen-nosed otter, following eagerly the scent where it had squirmed and writhed its way in the grass. The conger had stayed in the dyke, hiding in a drain by the flag-irises, and coming out when the colder salt-water had drifted down.

The marshman carried it back to his cottage, and cut it open, and then stared into my face with amazement and sadness, for within the great eel were the remains of his ducklings.

A CROWN OF LIFE

For five centuries Frogstreet farmhouse was thatched, the kitchen floor was cold and damp and uneven with slate slabs, and there was nothing to do on winter nights except to sit round the open hearth, on which all the cooking was done, and which smoked—nothing to do except go to bed, if you were one of the children, and listen to Father's voice mumbling through the floor, the whining of the new puppy shut up in the barn, cows belving for lost calves, the owls hooting in the trees, and the rain dripping from the thatch.

For five centuries the walls and the downstairs floors were damp and the rooms were dark. The yeomen Kiffts worked hard from before sunrise to after sunset during the four seasons; they possessed the lives of their sons, who worked, often beyond middle age, without pay, for their father; they shouted at and kicked their barking cattle-dogs as a matter of course; they thought nothing of beating, with their brass-buckled belts, their unmarried daughters if they stayed out late without permission; they went regularly to church on Sundays; and they died of rheumatism usually before the age of seventy. A small stream ran beside the wall, just below part of the kitchen floor, giving the place its name of Frogstreet.

2

When Clibbit Kifft inherited the property, it already had a mortgage on it, raised by his father because wheat no longer paid, owing to the importation of foreign corn; and

Clibbit was forced to raise the second mortgage to pay death duties. Then he married the young woman he had been walking out with ever since his mother had had her second stroke and died. Clibbit Kifft had hated his father, believing that the old man's wickedness had killed his mother. Clibbit had loved his mother dearly.

Clibbit's wife was a large woman, retaining through life the fresh red cheeks and brown wondering eyes which made her prettiness when Clibbit had been courting her. She had been sorry for Clibbit, knowing how, when a boy, his father had thrashed and worked him. His long swinging arms were said to be so loose because of the number of times his father had caught hold of him by the arm and swung him round before hurling him on the kitchen floor. As a young girl, daughter of Vellacott farm, she had pitied the poor young man with the shy and awkward manner. After his mother's death, when they were walking out together, he had never seemed to want to take her in his arms, but always to be clasped and held like a child. He was often querulous and moody for no reason that she could see, liable to leave her suddenly and not come near her again for days.

They walked out during the fall and winter, and when the warmer days came they went among the furze brakes on the coombe side and she was tender to him, and during that spring he was almost happy, often making her laugh with the way he imitated and mocked his father's ways; but when one night she told him they must be wed, Clibbit got into a real rage and shouted just like his father, before breaking into tears with the thought of what his father would do to him now that he would have to find a cottage and work for wages—saying that Father wouldn't have no strange woman about the place.

Father told him to go and never show his face again; but the parson helped Clibbit, giving him two days' work in the rectory garden—that made three shillings a week coming in—and lent him seven shillings to buy a pig. The parson also gave him an old bed and a table with three legs which had been lying for years in the disused rectory stables. Clibbit rented a cottage for fifteen pence a week, and the banns had been read in church—none too soon, said the neighbours—when Clibbit's father died without making a will. Clibbit had been an only child, otherwise the farm would have been sold and lost to the family a generation before it actually passed into the hands of strangers.

3

When Clibbit's fourth child was coming, Clibbit was past thirty, and growing just like his father in every way, said the neighbours; with one exception: the old man had been a limmer, drunk or sober, while Clibbit was sweet as a nut when drunk.

Clibbit's wife and his small children lived in perpetual fear of him. She never knew what he would do next or how he might appear. He might be home on time for his supper, the last meal of the day and eaten about six o'clock, or he might come an hour or two late, and find his plateful put back in the oven. He might eat it in silence; but he was just as likely to mutter that he didn't want no supper, then take it out of the oven, give it a glance, and declare that it was zamzawed (dried up), or not cooked enough, and tip it on the floor for the dog. Whatever he did, his wife would say little, but look at him and then at the silent children with apprehension. This look, and the unnatural stillness of the children, set him off in a proper rage; and as the time for her fourth confinement came nearer so his moodiness and fits of violence increased.

One Sunday's dinner-time he seized the tablecloth and pulled it off the table and set all the things clattering on the floor. He kicked the loaf of bread through the window, where it was sniffed out by the sow and promptly eaten with grateful grunts. After that he neither ate nor spoke for three days, except to reply, once, to his wife's faltered, "Won't 'ee have your dinner, won't 'ee, surenuff? 'Tes no use denying your stummick further," that he couldn't "afford to ait no more meals, what with all the mortgage money vor to be paid next quarter day". On the fourth day of his fast he came home mazed drunk, said the neighbours, who behind window curtains watched him lurching down the street, followed by his Exmoor pony; and they listened at their thresholds for noises following the opening and banging-to of the farmhouse door. Clibbit had had only a half-quartern of whisky, and after eating his supper and saying it tasted proper he slouched about the kitchen, smilingly patting his children's heads, shaking his wife's hand with beaming solemnity before taking off his boots and leggings, and going up over—to sleep exhaustedly in his clothes.

So the years went by. One August his eldest son—who had just left school being fourteen years of age—was sent to the inn for two bottles of beer. Returning with these, the boy jumped down into the field which they were reaping, and the two bottles, one held in each hand, clashed together and were broken. Unfastening the leather belt with the big brass buckle which had been his father's and grandfather's girdle, Clibbit roared out a curse and ran after the boy, pursuing him across half the field, whirling belt in one hand and holding up his breeches with the other. He stopped only because his breeches were slipping down. The boy ran on, and when he disappeared over the skyline, nearly a mile away, he was still running. The village thought this a good tale, and it was laughed over many times during the next few months—the beer bottles knacking together and young Kifft running like a stag over the skyline.

The boy never came back, finding a home and work with his uncle at Vellacott Farm.

4

Clibbit Kifft's appearance was remarkable. Village boys called him Oodmall behind his back, but never to his face. They would sometimes dare to jeer when he had gone round the corner riding his short moor pony. The intense wild blueness of his eyes under shaggy brows was instantly noticeable because of the long nose with its crimson tip. He was tall and very thin, a bony animation of long arms and legs in ragged clothes. His ancient cloth cap was so torn by brambles, as he knelt to till his gins and snares for rabbits, that only the lining and half the peak and shreds of cloth were left. Likewise jacket and breeches; and his leather gaiters were almost scratched away by his work.

Passing through the village on the way to one of his fields, riding the shaggy pony bareback so that his great nailed boots on the long legs almost knocked on the road, his sharp-featured head glancing about him from side to side, he appeared to some onlookers to be gazing about him like an oodmall—woodpecker. The rims of his blue eyes were always inflamed and his voice was like the yaffle's. The Adam's apple in his scrawny neck was almost as big as his nose. "Clibbit's throat would cut easy," the hen dealer would remark at cottage doors after one of Clibit's domestic rages.

The thatch of Frogstreet farmhouse was so old and rotten that docks, nettles, and grass grew out of the clumps of green moss on it. Oat sprays grew every summer, too, near the base of the chimneystack. The green waving awns of June always pleased Clibbit. " 'Tes ol'-fashion like," he used to say to the rector in his yaffly voice. " 'Tes wonderful old, thaccy wuts up auver. 'Twas me girtgirt-granfer, I reckon, laid thaccy wut reed up auver, 'cording to the records in the Bible box." Thatch was usually laid with wheat-reed, or unbruised wheaten stalks; oat or barley reed did not last so long as that of wheat. "Aiy, 'tes a wonnerful long time ago, when you come to think of it, Y'r riv'rence. 'Twas a master lot of smut that year, and the whate (wheat) crop was ruined, so they laid wut (oat) reed upalong. November, seventeen-seventy, George the Third's reign, I reckon, zur. A long time ago. Aiy. Wull, us'v all got to go sometime, beggin' riv'rence's pardon."

Everyone in the village liked the parson.

Rain went right through the remains of seven thatchings—the thatch was relaid four or five times every century, and the oat berry which sprouted and started a colony beside the chimneystack of Frogstreet farmhouse must have lain dormant in the roof for more than a hundred and sixty years.

Starlings, sparrows, and swifts made their homes under the eaves of Frogstreet, and every year a pair of martins built a mud nest over the front door, which opened on the road. In summer the stone of the threshold was continually being splashed by the clotted wreckage of flies, as the parent birds cleaned out their nest. Just like Oodmall, said the neighbours, "to be heedless of they dirty birds biding there"; but let it be remembered, now that all the life of that farmhouse is passed away, that Clibbit once said to the parson that the martins were God A'might's hens, which he liked to hear twittering there in the morning before he got out of bed.

When at last he was along; when his three sons had run away, one after another, at school-leaving age; when his wife, whose cheeks were still fresh and eyes candid as a child's despite her experience, had left Frogstreet finally, taking away the four smaller children; when the cows and horses and sheep and the last pig were gone; when the various inspectors of the Royal Society for the Prevention of Cruelty to Children, and the Royal Society for the Prevention of Cruelty to Animals, had paid their last visits; when for years no one in the village except the parson said a good word for the farmer, the martins were still there. It is unlikely that they were the original pair: so many long flights to Africa and back would have worn out those tiny hearts. Let it be thought that, although the old birds were long since dead, the impulse and desire to fly home to the English spring and the place of their birth was immortal. It lived on in the younger birds, and when they too were fallen, in their nestlings.

The soft waking twitter-talk of house martins in their nests before daybreak is one of the sweetest and happiest sounds in the world; and, although the woodpecker head was often poked out of the window just by their nest, the martins of Frogstreet farm never had the least fear of it.

5

"Aiy, Clibbit led bide they dirty birds," a village voice declaims, "but what about the long black pig Clibbit shot?"

"A raving bliddy madman was Clabbit," declares the voice; "a proper heller, that should have been stringed up long ago."

Yes, Clibbit shot a pig, a long black pig it was, that had been reared on a bottle by his eldest daughter. A sow died of fever, and the surviving seven of the farrow of little black pigs were placed in a basket before the kitchen fire. One of the elderly female cats that lived about the place attempted to adopt them, with an obvious lack of success which amused Clibbit greatly. Six of the piglets were fobbed off on Ship, the grey bitch who drove the cows to and from milking; her litter of mongrel pups had recently been drowned. She took to them as gladly as they took to her, and the old cat derived pleasure from helping Ship wash them. The other piglet was bottlefed on cow's milk and afterwards grew to the habit of coming into the

kitchen to see the eldest daughter, who had fed it, and also
to rout for and crunch in its jaws charcoal in the hearth.
Clibbit drove it out with kicks and blows, and the pig
learned to be absent whenever it heard his voice or
footfalls; but when, after listening and staring and snuffling, it thought he was not about, it would walk in and
begin its eager search for charcoal. It so happened that one
evening Mrs. Kifft put back Clibbit's supper on the
hearth, and the animal had just finished a baked rabbit
stuffed with sage and onions, a dozen potatoes, and a score
or so of carrots, when Clibbit walked in. He swore and
jerked his head about with rage, while the frightened
animal bolted behind his wife's skirts. "The withering
limmer!" roared Clibbit. "The flaming bliddy hog won't
ait no more zuppers nowhere, noomye! Why didden 'ee
stap the bissley bigger (beastly beggar) aiting vor my
supper, you?"

"I didden hear nor see nought!" cried the wife.

"You vexatious li'l loobey, you!" screeched Clibbit.
"D'ye mean vor say you didden hear no flaming bones
crackin'?"

"I did hear something, surenuff, midear, now you do
mention it, but I thought it was only th' ole pig, chimmering 'bout in they cinders, I did." She looked at him, her
eyes wide with fright, and the look as usual set him dancing and swinging his arms with rage, while he ground his
teeth and hit his head with his fists. Then, seizing the gun
from the nails driven into the lime-washed beam across the
kitchen ceiling, he whirled it round his head, took aim first
at his wife, then at the baby happily gnawing a carrot in the
decrepit perambulator in the corner, and finally pulled the
trigger when the barrel happened to be pointing at the
head of the pig. When the policeman, hastily summoned
from sleep and wearing his helmet, with his tunic im-
perfectly buttoned over his nightshirt, knocked at Frogstreet door and entered to ask sternly what " 't was all
'bout", Clibbit replied that he knew of no law against

killing a pig after sunset, and asked if he could sell him a nice li'l bit o' fresh meat.

6

Shortly after the incident of the pig shooting Clibbit was summoned to the Court of Summary Juridiction at South Dulton, the charge being cruelty to a cat, "in that he did cause it grievous bodily harm by compelling it to inhabit an improper place, to wit, a copper furnace of boiling water used in the process known as the washing of soiled domestic linen". Clibbit said he was sorry, and he looked it, and the chairman of magistrates, a prominent stag hunter, said he jolly well deserved to be pitched into boiling water himself just to see how he liked it. Fined two pounds or a month's imprisonment.

While Clibbit, his small head jerking about like that of a woodpecker starved in frost, was trying to say that he didn't have the money, a voice at the back of the court said, "I should like to pay the fine on behalf of my friend, if he would permit me." It was the village parson.

A woman cried out that such brutes should not be given the option of a fine, but should be flogged, and then be shut away in solitary confinement.

"Order!" cried a voice, while the clerk prepared to read the next charge. Clibbit went out of court, wondering what he should say to his reverence; but the parson was gone. He saw the woman who had cried out; she was waiting for him among a group of friends with blank faces; and she said, "We're going to watch you, let me tell you, and you won't get off so easily next time with your revolting cruelty. We know all about you, so you needn't think we don't!" He did not know what to say, but stood there blinking awhile, smelling of mothball, and jerking his head about, unable to look at any face; then touching his

1894 bowler hat—for he wore his best clothes, which also had been his father's best clothes—he muttered, "Yes, ma'am", and shambled away to where his pony was tied up. He would have liked a drop of whisky, but didn't like to go into any of the pubs lest he be refused.

So he went home and ploughed the three-acre field called Booaze (Blue Haze) until it was dark, having had no food that day. The kitchen was dark, the family in bed. He lit a candle and took down the gun from the beam. He sat down in a chair, the gun across his knees, and tried to cry, but he could not. The poignant mood passed, and he put the gun back, thinking that he would sell the calf next market day and pay back parson.

Clibbit did not sell the calf, nor did he pay back the two pounds fine. He avoided the parson, or rather he avoided the awkward feelings of gratitude and obligation, almost resentment, within himself by keeping out of the rector's way. He was in debt already, for he could not work the farm single-handed, and the fields were poor, the successive corn crops taken off them during the Great War, the land's fertility, not having been put back in the form of bullocks' or sheeps' dung. Farmers at that time were undercut by the importation of cheap foreign food; as a slight relief, they were exempt from paying rates and taxes on their land and farm buildings; but despite this, many small farmers were being sold up, noticeably those who, before the final smash, spent many hours every day at the inns. Weeds grew in their fields unchecked. Ploughs rusted in patches of nettles. Grass grew over and buried the harrows. Sales by Auction increased at Michaelmas and Ladyday quarters; but Clibbit farmed on. He had no other life; and that life was mortgaged.

7

At last Mrs. Kifft made up her mind for good and all, she told the neighbours; her brother at Vellacott had lost his poor wife, and was agreeable to have her live there with the children. All the neighbours watched the departure. Clibbit, after a couple of calls at the inn, helped load the boxes and perambulator on the long-tailed cart.

"What, be goin' vor leave your old feyther?" he squeaked to the baby, also called Clibbit, as Mrs. Kifft turned to give a last sorrowing look at the room, and the broad bed, with its wire mattress like a chain harrow, where her children had been born. Clibbit bent down and wriggled a scarred fore-finger at the blue-eyed baby. He saw the tears in his wife's eyes, and spoke loudly to the baby. The baby smiled at Clibbit. "Proper, proper!" said Clibbit. "Be goin' vor leave Oodmall, hey? Aw, I ban't chiding 'ee, midear!" he said in a serious voice, gazing at the infant, whose eyes were suddenly round. " 'Tes proper, 'tes right, vor you to go away. I ban't no gude. You go away, li'l Clibbit, and don't trouble nought about I. Go along, missus, your carriage be waiting, midear." Blinking the tears from her eyes, the woman went downstairs with the baby, and out of the house, and Clibbit was left alone with his pony, his dog, a pig, and two cows.

That night he spent in the inn, smiling and nodding his head and praising his wife in a voice that after four glasses of whisky became soft under its perpetual roughness. The neighbours remained silent. Clibbit told them what a beautiful animal was Ship, the grey longhaired sheepdog that followed him everywhere. "A master dog, aiy!" Ship's head was patted; her tail trembled with gratitude on the stone floor. They said nothing to that, thinking that in the morning the dog's ribs were likely to be broken by one of Oodmall's boots. Ship had long ceased to howl when kicked or beaten by her master. Her eyes flinched white, she crouched from the blow, her eyes closed, and a sort of subdued whimper came from her throat. She never growled nor snarled at Clibbet. Nor did she growl at anything; she seemed to have none of the ordinary canine prejudices or rivalries. Ship was old then. She was a grey shadow slipping in and out of the farmyard doors with Clibbit, or lying in the lane outside, waiting to fetch the cows for milking and returning behind them afterwards. Strangers visiting the village in summer, and pausing to pat the old dog, were likely to wonder why there were so many bumps on her ribs; explanation of the broken ribs was always readily forthcoming from the neighbours.

That evening Clibbit was drunk, but not so happy that he could not find his way down the lane to Frogstreet. He sang in the kitchen, and danced a sort of jig on the slate floor; the first time he had danced and sung since his courting days. In the morning he awoke and got up before daybreak, lit the fire, boiled himself a cup of tea, and ate some bread, cheese, and onions. He milked and fed the two cows himself, watered and fed the pony, and gave the pig its barley meal. Afterwards he and Ship followed behind the cows to the rough pasture in the marshy field called Lovering's Mash; all day he ploughed with a borrowed pair of horses, and towards dusk of the wintry day he and Ship brought the cows back to be milked and stalled for the night.

After more bread and cheese, he went up to the inn, drank some whisky, and then smiles broke out of his angular, tufted face and to the neighbours he began to praise wife, li'l ol' pony, dog, and parson. When he had gone home the neighbours said he was a hypocrite.

8

Clibbit's lonely farming became the joke of the village. He was seen pouring away pails of sour milk into the stream which ran beside Frogstreet and through the garden. He tried to get a woman to look after the dairy, but no one would offer. A letter written by an anonymous neighbour brought a sanitary inspector to Frogstreet; one of the cows was found to be tubercular and ordered to be destroyed. Clibbit sold the other cow to a butcher. He sold his sow to the same butcher a month later. His fields were overgrown with docks, thistles, and sheep's sorrel. His plough stood in one field halfway down a furrow, its rusty share being bound by stroyle grass whose roots it had been cutting when the neighbour had come up and taken away the pair of horses. This neighbour, a hard-working chapel worshipper, intended to buy Frogstreet farm when it came into the market, as inevitably it must. He was the writer of the anonymous letter to the sanitary inspector, and saw to it that everyone knew the property was worth very little; meanwhile he waited to buy it. Clibbit still worked at his traps, always accompanied by old Ship, getting a few shillings a week for rabbits. The neighbours said he didn't eat enough to keep the flesh on a rat.

The pony, already blind from cataract in one eye, and more than twenty years old, developed fever in the feet, and hoping to cure it, for he was fond of it, Clibbit turned it out into Lovering's Mash. It was seen limping about, an inspector came out from town, and Clibbit was summoned to the Court of Summary Jurisdiction.

The stag-hunting chairman of the bench of magistrates, after hearing the evidence of the prosecution, and listening without apparent interest to Clibbit's stammered statement, remarked that he had seen the defendant before him on another occasion. The clerk whispered up to him. H'm, yes. For the callous neglect of the horse, which with the dog was man's best friend—a most un-British line of conduct, he would remark—defendant would be sent to prison for seven days without the option of a fine, and the pony destroyed by Order of the Court. A woman cried, "Bravo, English justice!" in a shrill triumphant voice; she was turned out of court. The clerk read the next charge, against a terrified and obese individual who had been summoned for riding a bicycle at night without sufficient illumination within the meaning of the Act—to wit, a lamp—who said he had forgotten to light the wick in his haste lest he be late for choir practice. He led the basses, he explained, nervously twisting his hat. Laughter. Clabbit, following a constable through a door, thought the laughter was against him. He had not eaten for three days.

That night, Ship broke out of the barn, wherein she had been locked, by biting and scratching a way under the rotten doors, and in the morning she was found sitting, whining almost inaudibly, outside the prison gates. The sergeant of police on duty, recognizing her, said he would report the stray for destruction, but a young constable, to whom as a small boy Clibbit had once given an apple, said he would look after it until the old Wood Awl came out.

When he came out, his hair cut and his nose not so red, Ship ran round and round him in circles, uttering hysterical noises and trembling violently. Clibbit patted Ship absent-mindedly, as though he did not realize why he or the dog was there, and then set out to walk home.

Next day he was seen about his incult fields, followed by Ship, and mooning about, sometimes stooping to pull a weed—a man with nothing to do.

It was a mild winter, and the frosts had not yet withered the watercress beside the stream running through the small orchard of Frogstreet.

Three weeks before Christmas, Clibbit picked a bunch of watercress and took it to Vellacott farm. "For the baby," he said. His brother-in-law told him to take himself off. "The less us sees of 'ee, the better us'll be plaised," he said. "You and your outrageous cruelty! And I'll tell 'ee this, too, midear: us be puttin' th' law on to 'ee, yesmye, us be suing of 'ee into town, in the court, for to divorce 'ee!"

Clibbit went away without a word. His body was found the next day lying in Lovering's Mash, gun beside him, and Ship wet and whimpering. Watercress was found in his pocket. The coroner's court found a verdict of *felo-de-se* after much discussion among the jury whether it should be *due to unsound mind* for the sake of the family.

The neighbours were now sorry for Oodmall, recalling that he had been a wonderful generous chap sometimes, especially when drunk.

9

A week before Christmas the ringers began their practice, and the peeling changes of the Treble Hunt fell clanging out of the square Norman tower. It was freezing; smoke rose straight from chimneys. The first to come down the stone steps of the tower and out of the western door, carrying a lantern, were the colts, or youths still learning to ring; they saw something flitting grey between the elms which bordered the churchyard and the unconsecrated ground beyond. The colts gave a glance into the darkness; then they hurried down the path, laughing when they were outside the churchyard. But they did not linger there.

Others saw the shadow. The constable, followed and reassured by several men, went among the tombstones cautiously, flashing an electric torch on a heap of earth, still showing shovel marks, without flower or cross—grave of the suicide.

Frogstreet was dark and still, save for the everlasting murmur of flowing water; people hurried past it; and at midnight, when stars glittering were the only light in the valley, the greyness flitted across the yard and stopped, lifting up its head, and a long mournful cry rose into the night.

Towards dawn the cry rose again, as though from the base of the elms; and when daylight came the mound of earth was white with rime, and the long withered grasses were white also, except in one place beside the mound where they were pressed down and green.

The church choir, grouped forms and shadows and a bright new petrol-vapour lamp, went round the village, singing carols. Snow was falling when they walked laughing by the door and blank windows of Frogstreet, on the walls of which their shadows slanted and swerved. The girls laughed shrilly; Christmas was coming and life seemed full and good. Above the wall of the churchyard, raised high by the nameless dead of olden time, two red points glowed steadily. A girl ceased laughing, and put hand to mouth to stop a cry. In the light of the upheld lamp the red points shifted and changed to a soft lambency, and they saw the face of Ship looking down at them. "Oh, poor thing!" said the girl. She was kitchen-maid at the rectory. The cook told the rector.

The rector was an old man with a white beard, a soft and clear voice, and eyes that had often been very sad when he was young, but now were serene and sure. He had no enemies; he was the friend of all.

Late that night he went to the ground left unconsecrated by ecclesiastical law westwards of the elms and stood by the mound, listening to the sounds of the stream and feeling himself one with the trees and the grass and the life of the earth. This was his prayer; and while he prayed, so still within himself, he felt something warm gently touch his hand, and there, in silence, stood Ship beside him.

The dog followed him to the rectory, and touching the man's hand with its nose, returned to its vigil.

Every morning the rector arose with the sun and went into the churchyard and found Ship waiting for him, and his gift of a biscuit carried in his pocket. Then he entered the church and knelt before the altar, and was still within himself for the cure of souls.

10

On Christmas Eve the yews in the churchyard were black and motionless as dead Time. The ringers going up the path to the western door saw between the elms a glint and shuffle of light—the rays of their lantern in the icicles hanging from the coat of the dog.

And on Christmas morning the people went into the church while the sun was yet unrisen behind their fields, and knelt in their pews and were still within themselves while the rector's words and the spoken responses were outside the pure aloneness of each one.

With subdued quietness a few began to move down the aisle towards the chancel to kneel by the alter rail behind which the priest waited to minister to them. He moved towards them with the silver paten of bread fragments.

"Take and eat this in remembrance . . ." he was saying, when those remaining in the pews began to notice a small chiming and clinking in the air about them, and as they looked up in wonderment, the movement of other heads drew sight to the figure of the old grey sheepdog walking up the aisle. With consternation they watched it moving slowly towards the light beginning to shine in the stained glass of the tall eastern windows above the alter. They watched it pause before the chancel step, as it stood, slightly swaying, as though summoning its last strength to raise one foot, and a second foot, and again one more foot, and then the last foot, and limp to the row of kneeling people beyond which the rector moved, murmuring the words spoken in olden time by the Friendless One who saw all life with clarity.

The verger hurried on tiptoe across the chancel, but at the look in the rector's eyes, and the slow movement of his head, he hesitated, then returned down the aisle again.

The dog's paw was raised to the rail as it sat there, with dim eyes, waiting; and at every laboured breath the icicles on its coat made their small chimmering noises.

When the last kneeling figure had returned to the pews, with the carved symbols of Crucifixion mutilated in Cromwell's time for religion's sake, the rector bent down beside the dog. They saw him take something from his pocket and hold it out to the dog; then they saw his expression change to one of concern as he knelt down to stroke the head which had slowly leaned sideways as sight unfocused from the dying eyes. They heard the voice saying, slowly and clearly, "Be thou faithful unto death; and I will give thee a crown of life", and to their eyes came tears, with a strange gladness within their hearts. The sun rose up over the moor, and shone through the eastern windows, where Christ the Sower was radiant.

THE MAIDEN SALMON

Here lies the moor, wild with green bog and curlew's song in spring, grey with granite tors ceaselessly carved by the winds of centuries, the winds bringing Atlantic clouds which in the cold air over rock and valley fall as rain and fill many rivers flowing rapidly to the ocean again. In all the rivers, save those polluted by man with his mines and factories, salmon are born, and live their young lives awhile before migrating to the sea, to roam in deep waters where only death or dream has taken men; and after several years they return to their native rivers, in silver sea-dress, for the sake of love, to spawn; and nearly all of them die there.

One morning in the New Year a man was walking beside a thread of water which ran bright and clear under banks of carven peat. He walked on a path among rushes and granite boulders and soft green moss, a path used only by himself, by sheep, and wandering foxes. He walked alertly, hopefully, for the sun was shining and shadows of white billowy clouds were moving swiftly northwards over the moor. For weeks ice and snow had held down the life of earth and water; now the south wind was bringing hope and renewal with the sun.

Following his own path beside the runnel of water, he came into a wide valley made during hundreds of thousands of centuries by water hastening to the sea. Here under the hills ran the river from which the moor takes its name, one of the most famous salmon rivers of the south.

A score of paces before the junction of runner and river he stopped, and kneeling on a stone, examined something intently, his face near the water. When he looked up, his face was alight with joy: for one of the salmon eggs in the tray, made of stripped and charred withies of the dwarf willow, lying on the gravel, had hatched.

2

During the past summer this man, who was a poet and an ex-soldier, had cut a channel through the turf, and dammed the runner with boulders. A small pool was formed, and water flowed along its new bed. He made a wooden fender, which could be lifted to regulate the flow of water; and a box of fine granite gravel placed inside the fender acted both as filter for silt and screen against any fish or water-insect drifting down with the current. At the lower end of the new channel he set a wooden box with a grill made of an old pail, pierced with nail-holes, to stop entry from the river, knowing that eels and trout work upstream in search of food, especially if that food be salmon-eggs. An eel quests for and works the foodscents in a river as keenly as a hound after the quarry has been found.

Then in October the rains fell, driving and drifting like smoke across the moor; and when they ceased water cried night and day against the earth, faintly in trickle and string and bubbly splash through the peat hags of the higher ground, growing louder as it fell in rillet and cascade and swilling glide over and on the granite until it roared down the valleys, a dark-brown flood against which the salmon bored and leapt, as they journeyed upwards to the spawning redds at the river-head. The man watched them, identifying himself with them. Water-bailiffs, paid by the Conservancy Board to frustrate poachers with gaff, wire-noose, net, and bomb, soon ceased to be suspicious of him, as day by day he stood by the fish-passes in the weirs built along the lower beats of the river. To the watcher from the moor the fish were noble travellers, returning to the perilous river from the safety of Atlantic waters on the only true aristocratic impulse of life, the instinctive search for immortality through love.

Joyously the salmon were returning to the stream where during the first two years of their lives they had worn the brown, red-spotted dress of little trout—growing therein hardly as long as a man's hand; now, as mature fish, they rolled and played joyously under the weirs and waterfalls, strangely excited by the imminence of peril for love's sake. These fish feared shallow water, yet they swam on, boring a way up waterfall and torrent, often to be hurled back and pounded against rocks which bruised their bodies and broke their tails; or they clung with paired fins to certain jags which wore their scales away until the flesh was exposed.

The poise of a salmon, the power of its accumulated sea-strength, lies along its tapered length. Its flexibility is its life; it dreads each upward leaping into the stupendous solid power of water roaring over a high precipitous weir; it noses the water; it slides up and drifts back, exploring with its sensitive flanks, again and again, until its own golden power of faith returns unto its being, and it hurls itself out of the foaming pool and bores its way into that which gives it immortality . . . So the poet, lonely and proud in his own spirit, thought as he watched the autumn run of salmon ascending to the spawning redds on the moor. Weary beyond thoughts of crucifixion and resurrection, self-withdrawn in despair from the deathly ways of his fellow-men, libing beyond hope of human companionship since the realization in his thirtieth year that he had been born to love God, he yet lived and was upheld with Faith; and in some way, which he could not (nor indeed did he wish to) formulate, salmon were of that Faith. All he dare think to himself was that a fish was anciently the symbol of baptism, of rebirth, of Heavenly Consciousness. And did not Jesus say that this was Love— Jesus, whose tears were clouds these many centuries? With such strange and incalculable feelings the hatching bed was made in the runner, high up on the moor; and a handful of salmon eggs from the spawning bed in the river transferred there, carried in damp moss.

The eggs were the colour of Californian grapes, a faint pinky brown. Lying still on the bank, he had watched the male fish taking the female's place over the eggs: a pale cloudiness floating away in the water. A farmer had seen the fish there, too, in water less than nine inches deep, so that their black fins and tails were in air. Next morning the redd, or spawning bed, was empty. A pitchfork had killed the fish, and lifted them out, to feed the farmer's pigs in the farm on the hillside, a small grey building standing gauntly within a rectangle of starved trees half ruined by wind.

Very carefully the poet had put the eggs in a hatching tray, and covered them with a hurdle made of willow and mountain ash wands to shut them from light and the scrutiny of birds. Then came frost and ice, and for weeks his own life was suspended with that life developing within the eggs. At last the warm south wind brought a thaw, and he waited in the sunshine for his own renewal.

3

Against the lower end of the wicker-basket he saw the broken egg-covering turning and bobbing in the limpid flow of water, scarcely an inch deep, which twirled through the spaces in the wickerwork. It was like a very small colourless grape-skin. There in the corner, hiding, was the baby salmon—an alevin, luminously opaque, no longer than his fingernail, a mite with the egg sac still dependent upon it, now its belly. He touched it with the tip of a curlew's feather, and it wriggled swiftly across the tray with extraordinary speed. He felt his life glow within him, as he covered the tray carefully to keep the light from its eyes, and rising, sang as he walked down the path to his hut.

The next morning other eggs had hatched. With the curlew's feather he lifted the skins from the water, and several eggs which were an opaque yellow, sign that they were dead. The alevins wriggled rapidly, always head to stream, under the eggs, to get away from the light. One wriggled more rapidly than the others, and he knew it for the alevin that had first hatched. Every egg was rolled over delicately with the tip of the feather and scrutinized for the slight furriness indicating the fungus of disease. The wicker tray, with its bars of withy almost touching, had been charred in the flames of his hearth so that any fungus on them would be killed, and any underwater growth prevented. Water wimpled clear over the unhatched eggs and the semi-transparent alevins pressed between them.

Every morning he walked along the path by the runner, to watch over the alevins and remove the old egg-skins. After ten days all but six were hatched. These were still clear, they were infertile, and he lifted them up the side of the tray with the stiff edge of the feather and flipped them one by one over the lower screen. As the sixth egg struck the water there was a slight bulging rise, made by the head of a cannibal brown trout which for days had been waiting below the screen, drawn by the scent of salmon alevins. Seeing a blurred movement as the man stood upright, the trout sped away, making a ream or wavelet on the surface of the water.

At the beginning of the third week nearly half a hundred alevins were pressed together in one corner of the tray. The quickest of the alevins, browner than the others, was the one he always looked for; it was the first to be hatched, and already its sac was shrinking into its body, and in shape it was almost a little fish.

A water-snail wandered into the sanctuary, and although it was small its shell was several times the size of the holes in the screens. How came it there? He sought for

holes, and found one under the entry screen. He had
omitted to clear away grasses and rootlets which had
collected there, and this had caused the water to rise higher
and to fall through the holes, cutting a pit under the lower
framing of the screen. This he blocked with a turf, which
he firmly trod down. Afterwards he searched in the channel for any eel or trout that might have passed through.

Next morning, when he lifted the hurdle, he saw something that made him start with inward anguish, for against
the side of the wicker-tray lay a small fish as long and
broad as his thumb, with a squat ugly bull-like head,
mottled and spotted with brown. It squatted there, holding to a blackened cross-stick with fins like yellow hands.
And the right top corner of the tray, where the alevins had
huddled together, was empty. The dwarf fish, eater of
salmon fry, was alone in the tray.

The poet felt the doom of his previous life on the
world's battlefields, before he had sought purification by
solitude upon the moor, coming upon him dreadfully; and
he turned away with a gesture of weariness, and lay on the
sward with one arm outflung, while the water seemed to
be flowing away with his life, leaving it vain and purpose-
less as the sky which saw birth, growth, decay and death
with equal vacancy. He lay there while the shadow of
rushes in the south-running water slowly drew into the
bank, leaving the stream sunclear and glassy.

4

Footsteps brushing the heather made him look up, when
the footsteps ceased. He looked into the clear eyes of a
young girl regarding him with steadfast gravity. The sun
was behind her, her outline arose slender and shining out
of the moor. The flow of his life to the vacant sky ceased,
and returned to him as she came slowly nearer, her eyes

losing the firmness of their gaze as she approached, as though with doubt; yet their clarity remained. Lightly she came nearer, until she was leaning down over the narrow ribbon of water, staring at the tray with its misshapen occupant. Her clothes were poor and torn, her thin bare legs scratched with brambles, her mouth was large, her eyes were blue; probably she was, he thought, the daughter of the farmer to whom salmon were a means for cheaply feeding pigs and manuring vegetables; and his eyes lifted to the gaze of her blue eyes, childlike and calm with mental fearlessness, regarding him. They are gone, he heard her saying softly, and her eyes became wistful, and her gaze fell. A thought came to him, overlaying the thought of her candid eyes and brow, that by her remark she must have visited the hatchery, that she had put the mullhead in the tray—the ignorant and destructive ways of men were inescapable. Yes, he replied, and turned away from the sun.

She was gone without sound.

The water drew to itself a shadow from the bank, singing its song and bubble and swirl, green moss and white granite and gleam of sky, while a lark flew up and up into the blue, aspiring to the sun. The poet sat up, and looked sadly into the water, at the mullhead squatting there in the same place, replete, dull, gorged with its feast of the innocents. There was a glitter within the water as he shifted position. He peered down, and put his hand in the stream, to pick up a small piece of metal, star-shaped, that appeared to be, as he examined it . . . but was it possible? Gold? And how came it there? A gold star? Then he glanced down at the tray, where the dwarf had shifted when he had dipped his hand, and now was cowering in the corner; but it was not there he looked, but at a tiny fish which was poised, vibrating gently, behind the tail of the mullhead. He knew it for his own, and first-born, the alevin which now was a real fish, although scarcely more than an inch long, scaled, tapered for poise in water which

flowed from the rock! The mullhead darted forward, and
the little fish moved after it, keeping always behind its tail:
the triumph of reason over massive strength, David de-
feating Goliath, life triumphing over death; and the gold in
his hand was surely a symbol, a message of hope, like the
morning star before sunrise?

He scooped the mullhead, against which he had had no
feelings of anger or revenge, in his hand, and slipped it into
the stream below the grill. There was a swirl in the water,
and the olive-brown head of the cannibal trout showed in
an instant; and then the stream flowed placidly once
more.   .

5

Sweet summer lay over the moor, with cirrus clouds in the
height of the sky. Bees climbed happily among the honey-
bells of heather, and the murmur of water arose from
among the feet of the hills. In the mellow evening light
waterflies rose and fell over the river, dropping their eggs
from delicate long whisks below their gauzy wings; to fall
spent as the evening star glowed softly, the purpose of
their lives fulfilled, to die as dreams of twilight and the
everlasting compassion of death. The poet stood by the
hatchery, while the rings of trout dimpled the river, and
collected the tired flies, and let them drift, void of life, on
the glimmering surface of the channel. Gracefully the
samlet, with a slow sweep of tail, rose and lipped the
water.

When the leaves of willow and mountain-ash began to
turn yellow the samlet was as long as the man's little
finger, a taper of golden brown spotted with black and
red, and dark smudges, like thumbmarks, on its sides. It
wore the workaday dress of a trout, like all young salmon
while the Water Spirit prepares them for the deep waters of

the Atlantic where they alone of fish are noble; but its mouth was smaller than a young trout of its own size, its head more shapely. When the poet leaned over the channel, the little fish with a double fanlike wave of its tail-fin would swim up from the resting-place on the white gravel and take food from his fingers. When he was gone it watched the water moving past for daphne, shrimp, and nymph of hatching waterfly, buoying itself in the gentle current; or it slept, resting on the bed of the channel, against the peaty side, while its golden-brown colour dulled and its scales took on the hue of the peat. There it passed most of the winter, its being suspended with the life of the stream.

In its second summer it grew longer than the man's middle finger, and it could leap easily thrice its length into the air after flies hovering there.

Again at the fall water ran everywhere down the moor-slopes, gleaming grey with a sky of low and swiftly passing clouds. On a certain day and night in November rain fell with a heavy steadiness that appeared to overcome all other elements, and the conquering roar of the spate filled the misty valley. The path by the runner was drowned, the runner itself was now a river tearing down past the hut on the knoll with the speed of wild moorland ponies. For seven days and nights the rain fell, ceasing only to assemble new darknesses of clouds, and the level of the spate rose and dropped back a dozen times a day. Once when he looked from the door of his hut, hazy with the smoke of a peat fire, the man heard a sound of whistling like curlews crying, and saw the brown whiskered heads of three otters riding down on the flood, as they passed in their play of hide-and-seek amidst the unfamiliar hurlyburlies of the torrent. Rocks weighing many tons were undercut and rolled down the valley with dull bumping sounds.

And then the rain ceased and the weak winter sun shone again, and within a few hours the water was running clear once more. The hatchery was gone, the old channel filled with rocks and gravel, the screens washed away. Where was the samlet now? he wondered forlornly; perhaps in the sea, carried there before its time, or champed in the jaws of one of the cannibal trout which dwelt in the deep weir pools down the valley.

Yet the poet had faith; and in his belief he set himself to clear the choked bed and to reset the dam of boulders across the runner by the channel inlet. A stone was placed where the top screen had stood, and water pouring over this carved a pool where the samlet had lurked before. In February, when the first flies began to hatch—small stone flies which as nymphs had built each around itself a shelter of stone specks cemented together, with a doorway for their heads—he saw one morning a slight bulge in the water, and there, poised between the two converging flumes of currents, maintaining its stance with the least muscular effort, was his samlet, thinner and darker with winter fasting, but there it was, his darling fish, returned to him after the winter drear.

So April came again, with the willow's hair drooping silver and green, and a solitary swallow playing in the light airs of the valley, while from afar came the voice of the cuckoo. Every day the poet came from his hut, where he was writing an epic of the moor's ancientness and wisdom, to visit the samlet. In the last week of April it began to leap into the air and play on its side when it saw him. It became strangely excited as April ended her days. The golden hue of its scales gleamed brighter; it was changing its shape, too, growing longer, slimmer. Now the red spots were vanishing, and the black spots were as though washed away by the stream, which was laving it with silver! No longer was it wearing its moorland dress of a trout, but before his eyes the Water Spirit was fashioning for it a sea-coat of newest silver. No longer was it a samlet, but a smolt, scaled with argent armour for its adventure down the river to the sea, and that journey to Greenland, far from the submarine ledges where the last of Europe breaks away into the realm of deep waters, where only death or dream has taken men.

Knowing the hour was come, he lifted the smolt from the water, fixed the star with silver wire to the little shortened near fin on its back, and released it tenderly into the stream again. The next day the pool in the channel was empty.

6

Now every surviving Atlantic salmon, excepting an occasional straying fish, comes back to spawn in the river of its birth, from the northern feeding grounds of ocean. Scientists, who walk where poets fly, do not yet agree how each fish finds its particular way home. Some say they return by instinct. Of the Eastern Atlantic salmon, the short deep Tay fish returned to the Tay, the long lean Exe fish to the Exe, the heavy Wye thirty-pounder to that river which almost divides Wales. By instinct, say the scientists: every egg carries its potential sea-route. Innumerable generations passed up and down this river, the habit was laid deep, and eventually was put into the egg, like the habit feeding, breathing, swimming, and the deeper functions of gills, blood-course, and sight. This, they say, is instinct. By instinct the salmon returns. But the poet had seen eyed-ova of Tay salmon brought from Scotland to the extreme south-west of England, hatched in a Devon hatchery, planted as fry in a Devon river, and in time they returned, not to the Tay, but to the Devon river, short deep fish among the lean native salmon. There was, he knew, in the salmon a beautiful natural memory of place— pool, bend, fall, and quality of water—which to him was divine.

For nearly two years he lived and worked in his native cathedral city, inspired by thoughts and dreams of the fish which had gone down to the sea bearing the star of gold into the blue twilight of its ocean destiny. He was known to be queer from the shocks of battle he had sustained. His friends were sympathetic towards him; he realized that he had to make his own adjustment to living; but the passionate few alone saw beauty in his face, akin to that of mediaeval saints in old pictures, and recognized a rare quality in his poetry.

At the beginning of the second April after the smolt's departure the solitary young man was visited by a growing sensation of excitement and of the fateful imminence of an indefinable dread. After two years in the sea, he knew, the salmon would be between five and seven pounds in weight, and was likely to return to the river, a small spring fish. By the shape of the smolt he had known it was female. At that very moment his maiden salmon might be coming in from the Atlantic, travelling the route, with others of its generation, which would bring the schools east of the headland, along the shingle bank under the cliffs, and round the shore of the next headland to the estuary of the river.

The poet was almost to the climax of his epic, but he could write no further: he suffered mental anguish through doubt and confusion, which led to distrust of his inspiration, believing it to be self-delusion, his thoughts due to physical inactivity or frustration.

A line in his poem seemed to stand out of the page:

His tears are clouds since many centuries

and beyond that sorrowful truth he could find no pathway.

That night in sleep he dreamed of his salmon, which glowed with unearthly radiance in the night of his vision; and awakening, he dressed, packed his rucksack, took his staff, and set out on the road to the moor and the sea as the morning star was rising above the cathedral with its carved

stonework figures obliterated by the rains and winds of
seven centuries.

He walked throughout the day, resting at night at an
inn, and the next morning went on his journey, arriving in
the afternoon at the westward end of the shingle bank.
Returning salmon were cruising through water a few feet
from the shore, working round the coast, seeking the
river. And along that shingle bank, at intervals, were
fishermen with nets and boats, each waiting crew having a
lookout man posted on the cliffs above the ruin of a fishing
village washed away in one of the great storms which visit
the coast of the English Channel once or twice every
century.

7

For days the poet waited, concealing his anxiety; friendly
with the fishermen, yet aloof.

Sometimes, as he stood by one or another of the
watchers, he would hear a shout, see an arm pointing, cap
in hand, in a certain direction. Men would appear out of
the ruins of the village; they ran over the shingle; the small
boat was launched; a net shaken over the stern while two
men rowed vigorously in an arc towards where the
watcher was pointing. A shadow-shape moving east-
wards in the dim greenish water; a slim shape curving out
of the sea less than an oar's length from the beach, falling
back into its bubbled plunge and broken circle of whitish
bubbles vanishing. The widening surge of ripples had
hardly settled when the fish leapt again twenty yards
farther on, to fall and smack the surface of the sea, thus
hoping to rid itself of sea-lice clustered near the tail. Many
times the poet hastened down to the shore to see a fish
dragged in by the net; and he trudged from boat to boat,
asking permission to look under the squares of canvas

lying high up on the shingle, covering the day's catch of each crew.

On the seventh morning a new crew and boat appeared, rowed by an old man, his two sons, and his daughter. The poet watched her as they drew up the bow of the boat upon the edge of the shingle. The girl's thick fair hair, bleached by the sun, was clustered short on her shoulders. Her arms and legs were bare, golden-brown in the sun. She laughed with her brothers, tossing back her hair; she was strong in her sea-grace. The child he had seen by the hatchery four years before was now a woman. The poet stood there, still and silent, stirred by her beauty, his thoughts cloistered apart from that which was of the realm of dream. Then seeing him, the girl also stood still and silent for a moment, while he thought that never had he seen a brow so candid, or eyes so direct and clear, as though with the sky's clarity. A strange joy stirred in him.

A shout far away to the westward, another shout nearer, a third shout. There was excitement and movement among the boats on the beach. More shouting and waving arms from the cliff-watchers and crews alike: several fish had leapt at once. Again and again, leap along the shore.

One brother, wearing blue woollen jersey and sea-boots, remained on the shingle, holding the head-rope, while the boat leaped through the water, rowed by the girl and the other brother. Over the stern the father shook and loosened the folds of the net, which soon was hanging vertical in the water, between the row of corks on the headrope and the leads on the heel-rope. The boat de-scribed an arc to the line of shore, thus cutting off and enclosing an area to imprison fish. One after another, "lepping like greyhounds", in the words of the old man above, large fish jumped over the curve of corks as the seine was drawn ashore. Grey mullet. They stopped row-ing in disappointment. *'Twas zalmon I zeed, I tell 'ee!* roared the grey-beard, following his words with emphatic spittle. Then a salmon reamed along the water, and they bent to the oars again. The boat grated on the shingle, they jumped out and began hauling. The poet stood by, waiting with a feeling of his own life being drawn from him.

The net was hauled less slowly as the sea-drag lessened. The fishermen stared as they hauled hand-under-hand, heels dug into the shingle. The boat lifted and scraped gently at the water's edge. The last of the net, the long purse, came in rapidly. *Ah-aah!* One fish only. They were disappointed.

The poet's heart beat so that his body seemed hollow with noise, too weak to maintain itself standing. The solitary fish threshed the net in vain. A hand gripped it near the tail. It shook and curved, trying to escape. The poet saw a yellow sparkle in the sunlight, and his sight was instantly blackened.

The fish was carried up the shingle and dropped in a hollow amidst seaweed and the black horned shells of skate-eggs. There it writhed and writhed, seeking escape from the frightful elements of air and light. It was small-mouthed, silver-frosty, scarcely spotted—a maiden fish, said the fisherman, who did not notice the gold it bore on the small, pennon-like back fin.

It flapped and leapt and slapped down on the dry stones until blood broke out of the scales of the slender tail, and it weakened, fast losing its beauty, boring feebly, to lie still, dislustred; and after a while it leapt again, slapping away its life on the scalding shingle, seeking with the last of its strength to find the life which it had lost. The fisherman glanced casually at the figure of the man standing still by the fish, and then stooped to the re-piling of the net.

The poet stood beside the salmon, waiting during the agony and betrayal of the spirit's innocence by forces of life which he knew were irresistible and inevitable. And waiting there, he felt a strange joy arising through his pain, as he beheld the everlasting stream of time which flowed away from the world's end, to an immortal sea beyond the dusk of those great night suns called stars.

The salmon was scarcely breathing now. Slowly it lifted up, a curving sigh of farewell to its beauty; and it was ended.

The poet stood there, his eyes seeing not the steady glance of the girl beside him, nor anything mortal as he drowned in a sea deeper than the Atlantic.

8

Upon the shingle the breakers crashed, driven by the gale, to withdraw in white roar of foam. Far out beyond the estuary the sea was dark with peat water of the river in spate. Solid bends of swift water, brown but clear, hid the sills of weirs up the valley. On the hill above his hut stood the poet, watching the last of the sun sinking into the Atlantic, heedless of rain, lightning, wind. He watched dark clouds absorbing the last gleam and walked down to the lower ground, his head held high, his eyes steady and bright. His work was done, his life fulfilled, and now he might enter the everlasting stream of time beyond the end of the world. The river, faithful to the Spirit that breathed upon the face of its waters, creator of life through the symbol of baptism, should bear in the darkness his useless body to the sea's oblivion.

He entered his hut, and began to arrange papers, books, chair and cooking pots. The blankets were folded on the bed of ashpoles and bracken; the manuscript of his poem wrapped up, tied with string, addressed, left on the table. A note was written, giving these few belongings, and the use of the hut, to a younger poet whose work he had encouraged and helped into print. The fire on the hearth was sunken in grey ash and dull embers, a pale flame rising from the peat and sinking against the whitened stones of the hearth. Better to quench the fire before departing; but no, on this last night the virtue and service of fire should be treated with honour.

He sat before the wan flames hovering out of the peat, heather of olden time, that was yet sunshine and air and salt of the earth arising again in flame for the service of another form of life. The river's song arose in the night now glittering with stars, and he waited, serene and joyful in the ultimate triumph of poetry over the world. It became colder towards dawn, and he began to feel a return of doubt and terror; but he resisted the temptation to flinch. The flame was sinking, and soon he would be free to go.

And sitting there, his eyes closed, he rested in his spirit; and so fell asleep.

A pale visitant was now within the hut, revealing gradually table, walls, bed, floor, the poet's thin hands and knees and feet, the poet's face worn and tranquil, the eyes of which had dreamed beyond hope—the visitant revealed all as surfaces in one dimension: the visitant was Dawn.

Still in his dream, he saw himself getting on his feet and turning to the door. The door was opening of itself. A form appeared before him. Eyes of the sky's clarity looked into his eyes, and in her tender smile the sun's truth flowed to his being enfeebled by its long and lonely search in the moonlit land of truth. She was smiling, she came close to him, her eyes with the colour and truth of the sky. Her hand took his hand, and pressed it warmly. Her other hand was held open before him, with the golden star and silver link. His tears fell and he bowed his head, and she bent over him tenderly, and clasped him.

In the eastern sky the Morning Star, Eosphoros the Light-bringer, glowed with its white fires. Joyfully the song of water arose in the valley. The poet looked at his companion, and knew that his search was ended—for on that brow was the sunrise of a new world.

WHERE THE BRIGHT WATERS MEET

I did not want to leave Devon, I did not want to go away in the least, yet I was here on the station platform, watching the 9.1 a.m. London train approaching on the single line of the track. A ticket was in my hand. Basil stood beside me. I felt vague resentment that I was going to London on a Monday morning. Basil had to go back because of his business. He had an office somewhere in Westminster, and sold, or tried to sell, plaster-of-paris to builders. He had inherited the business from an uncle, and disliked it. Occasionally he came down to Devon to spend the weekend with me, bringing his fly-rod.

The train came into the small station, which was built in a cutting. It was a delightful place, with its little goods-yard, rambler roses on the platform, and oil lamp with bulbous glass globe in iron frame on a wooden post.

Basil glanced round and smiled his whimsical smile, preparatory to saying goodbye and thanking me for a most enjoyable weekend. I knew exactly what he would say. Basil was always punctilious and charming; his hair was always well-brushed, with exactly the right amount of brilliantine; his clothes were always neat, almost fastidious. He had been much ragged as a Guardee, but had done well in the war. The death of his father following a financial crash had brought him into the uncle's business—there was a warehouse of sorts, and a shortly expiring lease of a small wharf somewhere in the lower reaches of the Thames. Basil mentioned it with reluctance, with a shrug of the shoulders, and a slight smile.

"Don't let's talk about it, it's so perfect here in Devon. May I fish the Tree Pool after tea? Or perhaps you—?"

"My dear fellow, I can fish any time. But be careful of

Peter, won't you? No, do what you like. An otter or heron will get him if we don't. And if he goes away, he'll turn cannibal, of die of starvation, without the food he's used to. Get him if you can! *If* you can."

Yes, it was foolish to be going to London on a Monday morning. I had no real business in London; it could all be done by letter, anyhow. Basil held out his hand.

'Well, I wish I weren't going, my dear chap! It's been most awfully kind of you to have had me. It's probably an outrageous request, but may I come again, and soon?"

"Do, Basil. But I'm coming with you to London."

"Are you, really?" He seemed surprised, even puzzled. "That's splendid."

We sat down opposite one another. There was no one else in our carriage. I felt worried by his surprise.

"But surely you remember we arranged at breakfast to go to town together, Basil? You said you'd take me over your wharf."

He frowned in his polite, puzzled way. Basil would never contradict or disagree with anyone; he carried the oblique method of conversation to the nth degree of perfection. "Of course, I'd love to take you over the wharf again, my dear fellow," he said blandly.

"Again? What do you mean? I've never seen your wharf, Basil! You said less than half an hour ago that you had to meet a man there at three o'clock this afternoon, and when I said how the idea of living in an old Thameside wharf fascinated me, to get away from the family and write, you know, you said, 'Why not come up with me and see it?' You remember, surely?"

"Of course I remember, my dear chap! But"—again the whimsical look of puzzlement, "I could have sworn we discussed it a month ago, and you'd seen the place then. Of course I'd be delighted to show you the wharf, such as it is."

The train was getting under way; we were passing the trees of the Deer Park on our right. Soon the tops of the firs and pines were slowly lowering themselves beside us. The cutting was dropping away; the viaduct over the valley was in front. We were now above the blue-green tops of the spruces. We sat on the right of the carriage, peering through the open window for a sight of the winding moorland stream with its fringe of alders and occasional great oaks, and of the thatched cottage far away at the end of the valley. The noises of wheels on rails were increasing to a thunderous hollow: we were upon the viaduct, Suddenly I remembered the Bentley: why were we not going to London in the car? It was a 4½-litre supercharged model, and driving it was a pleasure. It was steady as a train at 80, 90, 100 m.p.h. Where was it? Had we left it outside the Ring of Bells the night before, when we had run up to the moor for a drink after dinner.

"Basil, where did we leave the car? I can't remember going home in it last night! We did go to the Ring of Bells, didn't we? Did we get very drunk, Basil? Am I still drunk? Is this a dream?"

"I've been wondering about that myself, my dear feller. Oh, look, there's the old grey heron, just alighting by the Tree Pool! I wonder if he'll get your big trout, Peter. Isn't the sun lovely on the trees! Look at the bullocks under the oak, beginning to swish their tails at the flies. Au revoir, river of bright water!" He sighed. "Why are we going to London on this heavenly day?"

We were now in the middle of the viaduct.

"Basil, I'm worried about the Bentley. And I can't remember walking to the station just now. How did we get there? Do you feel something queer—I say, who the devil are these two people down there, by the Tree Pool? Look, one of them is fishing! Damned poachers!"

"By Jove, yes! There's a spaniel with them, too. Calmly poaching! Probably they knew you were going to London."

"If only I could stop the train and get out! They may catch Peter."

We watched them in the distance. They were just visible beside the big hawthorn growing above the gravel ridge which floods had raised at the inner bend of the pool's tail. One of them was kneeling and casting; the other stood about a dozen yards behind him, out of the backward flight of the cast.

2

The viaduct of the Great Western Railway spanning the valley stands a hundred feet above meadowland and river. It rears itself on tall stone columns. I had often come here during the years of living in the thatched fishing cottage. One trespassed on railway property, of course, but that was part of its attraction. It was strange and fascinating to look down from that high place and see below one the slender tops of the spruce firs, where the wild pigeons had their nests. Jackdaws nested under the wooden sleepers bearing the weight of the shining railway lines; although they never appeared to have got used to the passing of trains, but flew out silent on black wings.

I became aware that the train was silent. It was at a standstill. Basil had opened the door, and had alighted. I followed him into the sunshine.

"We can go down through the trees, and then over the rushy ground without being seen until we're upon them," I heard myself saying, as we walked along the railway lines.

I moved in front of Basil. Rudeness, no doubt; but I was keen to get at those fellows below. I stepped rapidly from brown wooden sleeper to brown wooden sleeper, impatient at their short spacing, which curtailed a decent stride.

I scrambled down the steep slope by the first stone column, through the brambles and ash-plants growing in the rubble scree. A jump below, and I was in Farmer Coles's grazing, which was fenced with wire and posts from the Deer Park beyond. As I got under a loose strand of rusty wire I looked back for Basil, but I could not see him.

The two men fishing the Tree Pool were still in the same place when I peered from behind the oak growing on the bank above the gravel bed. Their forms were familiar, but I could not remember where I had seen them before. I was intensely interested in the way the leading man was fishing the tail of the pool. He was using my method of fishing in Devon streams, the unusual method of casting upstream with a single rough hackled fly on a fine tapered gut cast. Most fly fishermen fished with three wet flies downstream—tail, middle, and bob—and abandoned trouting when the water was low and bright; but this was the condition I loved, fishing upstream with a single dry fly.

One knew how a cat felt, stalking a mouse; every cast must be precise, the fly dropping lightly, its gamecock hackles glistening with the least touch of grease applied between finger and thumb, so that it rode high and airily on the slower water between stream and eddy where the fish lay. It was tiring work after prolonged writing at the desk, for one was taut and expectant, creeping catlike, all one's nervous energy in the eyes and wrist.

Now I knew that the man with the rod was drying his hackled fly by pressing it on a piece of *amadou*, that absorbent brownish substance made from a marine fungus. He was sitting on the edge of the gravel, among the young plants of docks and water celery. He lifted his rod, waving the fly backwards and forwards in the air as he pulled loops of line from the reel with his left hand. The fly sailed slowly, easily, to and fro over the water, until he had the length of line he required. I saw him tauten and the back of his head appeared to sink lower between his shoulders: he threw the fly forward with a deliberate slow intentness, while the movement of arm and shoulder, following the shooting of the line from a loop he had held in reserve, was perfect in its effect of slow-motion power.

I could sense the slow glide of the tapered and enamelled silken line through the agate and bronze rings. The line fell straight and aslant the direction of the stream, the lighter gut cast following after, and last to drop was the lure of silk and steel and feather. Almost as airily as thistledown it fell, to ride well-cocked on the water. From an underwater aspect the shining reddish hackles of the fly riding down imprisoned whirls of light; the shining skin of the water was crinkled but not broken. There it was, apparently a fat and juicy mouthful for any trout. I could feel the tenseness of the fisherman as I watched it, and when a blue-grey snout arose just where the water began to quicken into the tail of the pool, and sucked in the fly, and the fisherman gave a flick with his wrist that fixed the tiny barb into the corner of the bony mouth, I experienced an identical shock and excitement.

My tame trout, the three-pounder Loch Leven I had put into the Tree Pool a year previously, which had come by train in a carrier-tank from the fishery at Dulverton with a three-pounder brown trout, was hooked at last! I wanted to run forward, to demand furiously what they were doing there, but I remained watching. I noticed Basil kneeling on the gravel bank in front, and as the fish leapt he jumped up and ran forward. The man with the rod said to him excitedly, "You take the rod. I oughtn't to have done it". To my surprise I saw Basil take the rod, just before the fish dashed over the stickle below the pool's tail, and down the rough narrow water to the larger Viaduct Pool below. This was the trout's home, to which it had gone in its immense fear.

It fought as a hooked salmon behaves when it is red— that is, when it has been some time, perhaps four or five months, in fresh water, during which time it does not feed, but lives on its strength accumulated in sea-roving, waiting until the early winter when it will press up against floods to the top of its native river, where it will spawn, and perhaps die. A red salmon lacks the dash and surge of the clean-run fish. It bores, trying minute after minute to get to the bottom of the pool, there to avoid the terrible unknown enemy, usually invisible, which would drag it from the water. Gradually the unrelaxed pressure of the rod wears away its strength; it is confused, bewildered, beaten; it turns on its side, and is drawn to within reach of the gaff . . . That was how the big trout fought the lightest of rods and gut casts. After twenty-two minutes he gave up, showed his bluish-grey length spotted black and brown, his yellow-grey belly, the slightly hooked tip of his underjaw, as the net lifted him out.

3

Should he be returned to the river? Consider: he had been put in thirteen months previously, weighing three pounds; now he was two pounds two ounces. The river could not feed this great stranger from the fish-hatchery; the smaller, wild brown trout, of an average weight of four ounces, got the natural food—the hatching nymphs, the fallen duns and spinners—before him. For three years in the hatchery he had been used to the twice-daily scattering of artificial food—a sort of crushed and soaked puppy-meal and dried meat fragments. For another year in the river he had been awaiting in the Viaduct Pool the same sort of food borne down in the rough stream, whereupon he would move up to the tail of the Tree Pool and cruise around until the expected spoonfuls were cast from the familiar figure in the alder tree above him. The figure usually climbed the tree about noon every day, except when it was frosty or the river in flood.

The spring balance told his weight at two pounds two ounces. What would happen if the unnatural food supply were stopped? He would starve to death. He was probably a cannibal already, although when feeding with the smaller wild trout, which after months of suspicion had accepted the unnatural food, he had never even threatened one. It was an Utopian life while it lasted; competition was unnecessary when the benevolent deity from the sky scattered spoonfuls of manna for them. Even the tiny fingerlings, the yearlings trout and salmon-parr, hardly troubled to get out of his way, for while the daily shower lasted there was more than enough for all.

Two pounds two ounces; nineteen inches long; he had gone back a lot in condition. As for Paul, the big brownie which had been tipped from the tank with him a year before, a heron or otter had long ago had him. There were half-pounder Loch Leven trout in the pool, but they were quick and vital enough to feed in competition with the native fish; they were in marvellous condition, deep and fat like miniature Tay salmon, and their yellow-brown spots had changed to red—proof that they were nourished by natural food.

Poor Peter, there he lay, gasping on the stones, sometimes giving a desperate flap—a fish betrayed.

But if he were put back, he might go away, and, missing his food, become a cannibal, destroying hundreds of valuable yearlings.

The trout was grasped as firmly as possible across his lank and slippery middle by the left hand, while the right hand enwound with a handkerchief as protection from the prick of teeth, forced back the big upper jaw, until . . .

I tried to stop it; I ran to the edge of the water, crying out that he must not be killed, that the river and all it meant to my life would never be the same again if such a monstrous thing were done. He was my pet trout! He knew me; he would take food almost from my hand; he came up whenever I appeared on the bank of the Viaduct Pool, and waited there, expectant and confident. He must have trusted *me*, because if a stranger appeared on the bank he

would remain at his resting-place under the ledge of rock
at the pool's neck.

What words I shouted I don't know, but they were
shouted in vain. Under the pressure the trout's neck
cracked. He shuddered, and died.

I saw no more. In anguish I climbed the tree. The men
were gone. A heron was standing on the sandy scour,
where the visiting otters always scratched and rolled, ten
yards above the neck of the Tree Pool. From my perch,
where I had sat many hundreds of times before, I saw the
stones of the river bed through the limpid water. I saw all
the other fish I knew in their usual positions in the food-
stream flowing into the pool. The sunlight made the
brown and grey and blue stones, each with their clusters of
caddis shell-cases, clear and beautiful. I felt all the past
happiness of watching the stream return to me. And I
looked round the trunk of the tree, and its shadow thrown
across the shallow bed of the tail below, and there, in his
position behind the mossy rock around which the faster
water twirled, lay the big trout I called Peter.

4

He lay quite still, his belly resting on the gravel. His tail
was set in a slight curve against the press of the current.
There was a dark stain over the back of his head and
shoulders. He breathed slowly, like a trout asleep. I could
just discern the red of his near gill as it opened.

A hatch of fly was coming down. All the fish I knew
were at their stations in the neck of the pool, in the stream
itself swirling gently into the pool, and at the tail. Above
the neck, where the heron stood, the water ran evenly
round a bend, the bed of which was made of large stones
grown with water moss. The stones were too heavy to be
rolled by floods, and so they made a permanent hold for

the water moss, which in turn was good holding for various crawling *larvae* or nymphs of the ephemeral flies. It was a hatch of the Iron Blue duns. The mature nymphs, their future wings formed and folded within their larval skins, were leaving the shelter of the moss where they had lived for the past year. What excitement as they ventured the stream, prepared to quite one element for another!

The run carried them into the pool, where the trout were waiting, the biggest fish in the best positions. I saw them, ranged alongside and behind one another, undulating their bodies and expelling water through their gill-covers as they drove forward gently against the current, thus keeping position, while balancing themselves with back, pectoral, and tail fins. The wimpling surface of the water was immediately disturbed by the rises. Those in the run were bulging rises, caused by the fish moving up to take the nymphs above them—for a feeding trout looks forward and upward. Those nymphs which were not taken passed into the broader, slower stream, and reaching the top of the water, struggled to break their confining skins at the thorax. There other trout rose to take them, sending out elliptical ripples which the flow smoothed away.

Those nymphs which passed the suction of opening mouths broke their shucks, and, standing up in them, unfolded their wings with miraculous speed, dried them quickly and arose into the warm air as duns. I watched some seeking shelter among the leaves of the alders, where they would wait and cast their drab wing-cases and body-covers; to fly up into the sky of late afternoon for their nuptial dances: to descend, and to drop their eggs upon the surface of the water: to sink exhausted into the stream again, and then—whither?

A hatch of fly, and the consequent rise of fish, was a sight I had never ceased to watch with thrilling excitement. The river was alive, its multitudinous life in balance under the sun! My nature drew life from the living water.

While I was watching dreamily, feeling myself suspended as a spirit of water, the heron peering from its stance on the scour lifted its long neck and held up its head anxiously. Soon I heard voices from the direction of the farm-road under the viaduct. The bird flew up, passing within six feet of where I sat immobile on my perch of branches. It was curious to watch it folding its spindly legs straight behind its tail and tucking its neck between its shoulders. It flew past me, in its alarm apparently failing to see me sitting there, less than a yard from it.

5

The voice came nearer. I recognized the man who lived in the lodge up the river, his son and wife, and Farmer Coles, the tenant of the rough grazing fields beyond the viaduct. They were dressed in their best clothes of dark material. The men wore bowler hats. I kept quite still as they approached. They were talking about the fish. They did not notice me, hidden by leaves and branches against the trunk of the alder.

"That's where it was," I heard Farmer Coles saying. "I seed'n often. Great big fish 'e was. There, behind that stone, only you can't see the stone now as the sun be shining on the water. I could've had'n out with a rabbit wire on an ash pole if I'd a mind to, many a time, but I like a bit of sport myself, and he seemed a nice sort o' feller once you got to the right side of 'n. Perhaps it would've saved a lot of trouble if I'd yanked'n out, tho'!"

They spoke for a minute or so, and then, declaring that it was nearly noon, and if they weren't early they wouldn't find standing room, they continued their way down the farm-road towards the Deer Park.

I felt that I could sit in the tree forever watching the fish in the water. I saw Basil walking slowly on the bank by the

Viaduct Pool below me; and, getting down from the tree I went to him. He looked rather depressed, but smiled when he saw me.

"I say, old chap, has it occurred to you that something appears to have happened?"

"Well, now that you mention it, Basil, I must say I feel, well, rather—peculiar."

"You know the feeling one has before one realizes that one has 'flu? That exactly describes it. I think I'll go back to the house, if you don't mind, and rest in the shade."

We went home together, speaking occasionally, answering one another in monosyllables. The sunlight seemed harsh. It seemed to be beating like the clangs of great shining cymbals. Once or twice I felt a queerness in my progress, a distortion of the sense of balance. It was as though I were moving through flashing brass bars of dreadful sound. Through the plangent dissonance of life I noticed that many cars were drawn up outside the house.

"Something's happened, Basil. Keep by me. I feel so queer."

"So do I. God, my head aches."

He swayed. His face was very white. Vaguely I noticed two policemen standing by a six-wheeled lorry, on the body of which lay the remains of a smashed and burnt-out motorcar. I took Basil's arm, and we walked up the path by the hedge to the house.

It was packed with people. What were they doing there? It was an intolerable invasion of one's privacy. I remember complaining querulously to Basil, and that he did not seem to hear me.

Men and women, most of them strangers, were standing outside the open windows of the sitting-room. It looked like an auction. There must be some mistake. I tried to speak to one of the men crowding round the door, who were all peering one way. They were pressed too close together for me to get into my doorway. I thought of my wife, of my children. Where were they?

"Basil, what ever has happened?" I managed to say, through the hideous clanging sound of light.

Someone was speaking inside the room. I listened. It was the voice of the landlord of the Ring of Bells. He was describing a visit to his inn by two men in a motorcar.

"One on'm, the gennulman that writes books, had a master g'rt trout in a basket, sir. I heard tell of that fish—many had seen'n lying in the big pit below the viaduct. I gathered that the gennulmen who had the fishin', the writin' gennulman had caught his tame fish, and was very sorry he had done so. He said it was too thin, as far as I minds it."

"How much did he have to drink?"

"'Twas a couple of whiskies, sir. It may have been three. I can't swear to it. Maybe it was four. The gennulman seemed very upset because he had caught his pet trout and killed it instead of puttin' it back in the river. But it was no case of drunkenness in my house, your honour. What happened afterwards was pure accident."

"That is for this court to decide. I want you to say only what you know, from your own observation. Were the whiskies, as you call them, were they half-quarterns, what is generally known as doubles?"

"Doubles, sir."

"You mentioned four. Are you certain of this number? You also mentioned a couple, and also three. Evidently you are uncertain. Did they offer you any drink, by any chance?"

"Yes, sir. I had one to drink the gennulmen's health with."

"I see."

Other voices. I recognized my solicitor speaking. Then Dr. Bennison. Basil seemed to be very ill now, as he clung to my arm. I felt wretchedly sick myself, with a most ghastly headache. My eyeballs seemed to be flaring. If only I could get in out of the harsh sunshine beating on my throbbing head. I think I was beginning to lose consciousness. Very remote sounded the voices. I heard, in a series of swaying recessions, the words—blazing headlights—seventy miles an hour, or maybe eighty—a terrible noise as the car crashed into the telegraph pole at the bend of the road, breaking it in two—the car turned over and over, and burst into flames—charred almost beyond recognition.

Basil heard, too. He smiled at me.

We sat by the river, in the shade of the beeches near the waterfall. We did not need to speak. It was so peaceful, watching the shallow stream rippling over the ford, where the white flowers of crow's-foot on long green bines were ever waving in the current seeking to drown those slender lengths. The grey wagtail flitted from stone to stone, the dipper sang its rillets of song. The bright waters flowed to the sea and the sky, I with them.

ENGLAND HAVE MY BONES

In *England Have My Bones*, T H White, author of the classic *The Once And Future King*, describes a year spent in the English and Scottish countryside.

Written in 1934, *England Have My Bones* beautifully captures the rhythm of the passing seasons in a rural Britain now fast disappearing. And above all, it is a book that conveys the delight of country life as White pursues his own passion for fishing, hunting and shooting.

'I wish I had time to read this book instead of having to review it. By "reading" this book I mean taking it in little doses, poring over it, having it by one's bedside, cherishing it. It is a little like Izak Walton's *Compleat Angler*, Gilbert White's *Selborne* and Cobbett's *Rural Rides* . . . It is entrancing.'

James Agate

NATURE IN DOWNLAND

W H Hudson, author of A SHEPHERD'S LIFE, has long been one of the best loved chroniclers of English country life in the last century.

In this book, first published in 1923, he gives us his delightful reflections on the changing countryside of 'the threshold of England', the Sussex Downs. Hudson vividly portrays life in the small villages of Sussex with their lively, often idiosyncratic, characters while his naturalist's eye captures the rich landscape and wildlife of the Downs. No revealing detail of humour, character or beauty escapes his attention in this vivid and unsentimental picture of Downland life at the turn of the century, which will be read and enjoyed by all lovers of nature and of our rural heritage.

THE TOILERS OF THE FIELD

Born in Wiltshire in 1848, Richard Jefferies is now established as a classic writer of the Victorian countryside. Perhaps only Wordsworth was able to evoke nature in its many moods and feelings as Jefferies does, but combined with this lyrical feel for the countryside is an intense interest in the everyday lives of country people, but at work and at home.

The Toilers of the Field, first published in 1892, brings together Jefferies' finest work. Whether writing about the farmer at home, the daily life of a Wiltshire labourer, or of a typical English homestead, Jefferies creates a unique historical view of English rural life in the last century and a delightful picture of the changing rhythms of nature in the countryside.

GILBERT WHITE

First published in 1928, Walter Johnson's account of the life of Gilbert White has long been regarded as the classic biography of the great eighteenth century naturalist.

Drawing extensively on Gilbert White's diaries and letters, Johnson produced a fascinating and detailed picture of the naturalist's life which will be read with enormous pleasure by all who have come to know and love *A Natural History of Selborne*.

As an authoritative account of White's life and of his pioneering work as a naturalist, Johnson's biography has yet to be surpassed; but it also captures in full the delight Gilbert White himself took in the ever-changing country-side and wildlife of Selborne.

All Futura Books are available at your bookshop or
newsagent, or can be ordered from the following
address:
Futura Books, Cash Sales Department,
P.O. Box 11, Falmouth, Cornwall.

Please send cheque or postal order (no currency), and
allow 40p for postage and packing for the first book
plus 18p for the second book and 13p for each additional
book ordered up to a maximum charge of £1.49 in U.K.

Customers in Eire and B.F.P.O. please allow 40p for
the first book, 18p for the second book plus 13p per
copy for the next 7 books, thereafter 7p per book.

Overseas customers please allow 60p for postage and
packing for the first book and 18p per copy for each
additional book.